SHY AND MIGHTY

Nadia Finer is on a softly-spoken mission to help shy people be more mighty. She's the host of the Shy and Mighty podcast and a coach specialising in shyness. She has spent the last fourteen years helping people of all ages overcome their fears and insecurities so that they can step out of the shadows and achieve big things, without changing who they really are. She has travelled the world, speaking at international conferences, and has appeared in the *Guardian*, *Telegraph*, *Independent* and on Radio 4 and BBC Radio London.

SHY AND MIGHTY

Nadia Finer

QUERCUS

First published in Great Britain in 2022 by Quercus Editions Ltd
This paperback published in 2023 by

QUERCUS

Quercus Editions Ltd
Carmelite House
50 Victoria Embankment
London EC4Y 0DZ

An Hachette UK company

A CIP catalogue record for this book is available from the British Library

PB ISBN 978 1 52941 270 3
Ebook ISBN 978 1 52941 271 0

10 9 8 7 6 5 4 3 2 1

Typeset by CC Book Production
Printed and bound in Great Britain by Clays Ltd, Elcograf S.p.A.

Papers used by Quercus are from well-managed forests and other responsible sources.

SHY AND MIGHTY

SRY AND MIGHTY

For the quiet ones

CONTENTS

HELLO THERE

Shy people are the silent potential in every room.

When I was a little kid, I watched a black-and-white film called *The Invisible Man*. It frightened me to death and gave me bone-chilling nightmares for years.

Scary dreams aside, however, the idea of being invisible is very appealing to a shy person like me. Imagine being able to slink around without having to engage in small talk or worry about people looking at you. We could just lurk in the background, doing our thing without being picked on or put on the spot. Perfect.

In the absence of a fully functional invisibility cloak, I've had to resort to alternative measures. Sliding under tables, diving into bushes, hiding in bathrooms and wearing disguises. Being shy can get pretty weird.

We shy people love to blend in. We don't like confrontation and we find standing up for ourselves trickier than walking a tightrope in a high wind.

When I was eight, my primary-schoolteacher, Mrs Moore, was a relic of a bygone era. She was a handwriting obsessive, who believed that everyone should write with their right hand. She was convinced that handwriting, and life in general, should be straight and uniform.

My handwriting was a lot like me; small and curly. I am left-handed, and couldn't seem to make my writing stick up straight. One day, we were writing stories. Mrs M was not happy. She ordered me to write my whole story out again, straighter. It felt like she was ironing out my curls and loops, and my spirit.

I said nothing. I tried my best, but no matter how hard I tried, I couldn't make my handwriting stand up. Nor could I stand up to her. I had so much I wanted to say, but I couldn't speak up. I just didn't know how. I squashed my feelings down and slunk out to the toilet where I hid for what seemed like an eternity.

Hide and say nothing. That was my solution. In fact, it was my whole approach to life.

Another time, in the dorm room on a school trip, I couldn't sleep. *Someone is snoring*, whispered the girls near me.

I knew it wasn't me because I was wide awake.

It's Nadia.

I said nothing. I pretended to be asleep. I couldn't speak up.

They carried on talking about me. On it went. And I couldn't say anything. The longer it went on the more awkward it was.

But until I really did fall asleep, I stayed silent.

Hide and say nothing. Hide and say nothing. And repeat.

That just about sums up shyness.

I was fourteen when I first realised there was something a bit odd about my voice. It was in a French lesson, and we'd just got these fancy new cassette machines. You spoke into the headset and recorded your voice onto the tape so you could listen back to yourself and check your pronunciation. I loved French, despite my appallingly British accent. So, I happily recorded myself and then pressed play.

All I could hear was this little kid talking. Who the heck was that? And how come they were saying exactly what I had just said?

It took me a moment to understand that it was me. What the . . .?!

I sounded like I was five years old. How on earth had I not known this before? Why had nobody ever mentioned it?

I felt like my world had imploded.

I was devastated. I was a freak.

If I was shy before, things were about to go next level.

From that day on, I vowed to keep this little voice of mine under wraps. Essentially, I hit the mute button on my life. Under no circumstances would I put myself out there to be exposed to potential public ridicule. If I could have communicated solely through the medium of mime, I would have done.

My voice is still perfectly suited to cartoon voiceovers, as total strangers seem to take great pleasure in pointing out to me on a regular basis. (Thanks for that.) And sounding like this has made me feel self-conscious, awkward and shy – in the extreme.

I hate getting into situations where I have to speak.

Like the time I tried to book a swimming party over the phone for my son's ninth birthday. The woman on the phone thought I had stolen my mum's credit card and was attempting to fraudulently book my own birthday party. That incident raised so many questions in my mind. Like, who are these scamming nine-year-olds committing credit-card fraud? And what world does this woman live in that that was her first assumption? And how rude do you have to be to accuse someone who is trying to pay you money of a white-collar crime? And . . . Breathe.

Over the years, I've avoided so many things. I've avoided phoning people I don't know, leaving voicemail messages, having difficult conversations, standing up for myself, negotiating, sharing my opinions, saying yes to opportunities. I've avoided making videos, doing interviews, giving talks, entering competitions and pitching my ideas. It's a long list!

I've carried my shyness around with me like a heavy blanket, slowing me down and keeping me hidden. Dragging this blanket around is not conducive to meeting new people, sharing brilliant ideas and opinions or having crazy amounts of fun. It's debilitating.

For years, I have let my shyness control me. It's squashed and silenced me and kept me locked inside my own head. Rather than leaning in, shyness has caused me to stand back and watch as other people achieved great things; things I knew I was perfectly capable of doing too.

Life under the blanket of shyness is safe and warm. But it's also sad and lonely. And boring and frustrating.

If you are shy, you struggle to speak up, to convey your ideas and to get involved. It can feel like you're creeping around in the background of your own life. Like you're the invisible man (or woman).

Shyness is a bully.

And apparently not content to have my own personal bully living inside my head, I've also welcomed actual bullies into my life. I've been bossed around and walked over, let my boundaries bend beyond belief and been left in a messy heap on the floor. More than once.

Like a bully, shyness controls and isolates us. It causes us to miss out on fun, opportunities, friendship and success. We miss out on life. It keeps us small. It makes us feel like we are not good enough, that we are broken. And shyness also makes us feel alone.

Until now, being shy has been like being in some kind of secret society – so secret that not even the people in the shy society talk about it.

But we are not alone. Turns out, there are loads of us. Around half of all humans are shy. I bet you didn't know that. Still, we don't talk about shyness. Because we're shy!

For years and years, I didn't understand my shyness. I struggled to articulate what I was feeling, or why. I just knew that some things were not for me. And that even basic interactions could be a struggle, from ordering food to making phone calls.

And, of course, I never spoke about my shyness either.

Shyness needs a rebrand

Shyness has had a lot of bad press. Until now, it has been the shameful little secret we keep tucked away. Owning up to it feels like an admission of weakness or a childish lack of social skills.

But, why? What if, instead of seeing shyness as a flaw, or a personality blip, we start to see it as a quiet strength instead? What if we actually embraced our shy power? *Because we are not broken.*

Shyness does not need a cure. I mean, how can half the population be broken? Why should half the population need to change their personalities to fit in with the ideal of being outgoing and confident?

We shouldn't.

Rather than going for a full-on personality transplant, what if we learned to work with our shyness instead?

We shy people have so many skills and talents. We have sleuth-like abilities to understand complicated situations, ninja-level concentration skills, amazing amounts of empathy, creative brains buzzing with ideas and finely tuned listening skills. And that's just for starters. If you're shy, you don't need fixing. Or to change who you are. You need to be *more* you.

Success is equated with confidence, and the people held up as being successful – those who speak in public and on TV, launch new endeavours, get promoted, lead teams, organisations or even countries – are portrayed as extroverts, comfortable with visibility and self-promotion. And because these attributes don't resonate with shy people, success can seem elusive to us.

But shyness can be an advantage. It's rational and sensible to want to observe and listen and pay attention before you jump in with two big toe-capped boots and stomp all over everyone. Maybe instead of us becoming more like them, outgoing alpha-type people could learn from us?

I think it's time we hit that unmute button because, honestly, there are enough loud, dominant voices out there. And there's not much listening going on.

Unleashing the silent potential

In a culture where the extroverts dominate, quieter people stay, well . . . quiet, and our brilliant ideas and thoughts are lost. Quieter voices are missing from the conversation in business, politics, organisations, institutions, and society as a whole.

Unless we feel safe and supported, shy people will continue to hide, and the silent potential in our society will stay silenced.

The world needs a mixture of personalities, perspectives and skills to function and get things done. If shy people are under-represented in society, the only voices we will hear are the loud, shouty ones.

We need a range of voices, not just the loudest

And that's why I decided to write this book, instead of hiding away at home under a blanket, watching Netflix, with my fuzzy dog, Bobby. To give shyness a voice. Shy and mighty: that's the goal. Shy power!

All shy bods are welcome

This book is for anyone who feels shy.

Maybe you're a little bit shy sometimes, or maybe you're super shy all the time. Maybe you're not sure what's going on with you, but you have an inkling that shyness is the thing. Maybe you're sixteen or sixty. Man, woman or gender non-binary. This book is for all of you.

It doesn't matter whether other people think you're shy or not. This book is for you. And, believe me, everyone will have an opinion on your shyness. And guess what, we're going to ignore all of them. Your shyness is personal. It has nothing to do with anyone else. Zilch. Zero. Nada.

Perhaps you're not shy yourself, but you're seeking to understand shyness to help the shy people in your life. Maybe you're the parent of a shy kid, or you work with shy people and you want to help them shine like the superstars you know they are. Maybe you're a shy ally. This book is for you too. So, hey there, one and all. Welcome aboard!

About this book

I realise I might sound like a football pundit here, but this is a book of two halves.

The first half of the book will help you to understand your shyness: why you feel shy, what causes it and the impact of shyness on your body, your brain and your life. It's the psychology of shyness. Shycology, if you will.

Preachy self-help books are not my thing. I'm also not into super-complicated books that require weeks of study or a PhD to make sense of. The best self-help books are memorable. Their key idea can be distilled down into a golden nugget of brilliance. When you put the book down, you remember what the heck it was all about. And there will be one or two things you're going to do differently in your life as a result.

That's why at the end of each Shycology chapter, I'll give you a brief summary – one or two key takeaways for you to remember. That way, if you need a quick recap or you're in a rush, you can just skip ahead and get the shylights.

The second half of the book is focused on Shy Power. Our goal is to go from invisible to invincible. Each chapter will help you work *with* your shyness, taking little steps towards unleashing your potential, stepping out of the shadows and living a bigger life. Together, we are going to discover levels of mightiness you had no idea were inside you.

At the end of each Shy Power chapter is a Mighty Mission for you to action. These little steps will build up, and, over time, you'll emerge a more mighty version of yourself. But even if you only do *one thing* differently, your life will be that little bit more fulfilled and mighty as a result.

Want the short, short version right now? Well, here's what I want you to take away from this book – the key principles of Shycology. Our manifesto, if you will.

THE SHY AND MIGHTY MANIFESTO:
FROM INVISIBLE TO INVINCIBLE

- Shyness makes us feel isolated. But we are not alone.
- Shyness is not a shameful secret. Own it. Talk about it.
- Shy people are not broken. We don't need fixing.
- The ideal of being outgoing is not ideal. It's time for a softer, more considered approach.
- Shy people have unique qualities and skills. Nurture and appreciate them.
- Shyness is not weakness. We are mighty inside.
- We are the silent potential. The world needs to hear our voices.

Throughout the book are contributions from shy people talking, often for the first time, about their shyness. Some names you'll recognise, and perhaps be surprised to see they're shy, while others are people who felt it was time to finally speak up about their shyness to show that you're definitely not alone.

Any book that promises to cure you of your shyness should go straight in the nearest bin, as far as I'm concerned. I'm not going to tell you to change who you are or to put on a front every time you open your mouth. That would be terrible. Oh, and I'm not going to sit here, perched on a shiny pedestal, wittering on about my journey and how I overcame my shyness and am now wildly successful. I know how irritating that is. Besides, I would be lying. In founding the Shy and Mighty movement, in writing this book and talking to loads of shy people, I've been building my mighty muscles gradually, and I'm meandering my way towards becoming more mighty, slowly but surely.

In my opinion, you're wonderful just the way you are. But if you want to overcome certain aspects of shyness that are holding you back and learn to embrace the positive side of it, then you're in the right place. The best kind of change is a simple shift that feels natural and easy.

So, read on, oh shy one, and let's get to work.

SHYCOLOGY

CHAPTER 1

SHY SCHOOL

I don't mean to look like a bitch, but I get completely paralysed with shyness.

Keira Knightley, actor*

The first thing that happens when I mention my work on shyness to people is a stream of questions. And all these questions can feel like a police interrogation, with a desk lamp glaring in my face.

It turns out that shyness is way more controversial than I could ever have imagined, which, frankly, is hilarious, given the mild nature of the topic.

Shy people are often misunderstood. Outgoing people just don't seem to get us. To someone who is loud and outgoing, a shy person can seem arrogant or aloof, unfriendly, disinterested, bored, cold and switched off. They can also assume we're a bit dim, have nothing to say or that we are not engaged.

At the start of my exploration of shyness, I did not expect it to stir

* https://www.hindustantimes.com/entertainment/keira-is-shy-not-bitchy/story-yEhH-3veVhc8hIEu27g52LO.html

up so many weird vibes or so much uncertainty. But shyness can be a bit of a slippery fish. It's not something that is clearly defined, openly discussed or well understood.

That's why I think it's a good idea to get a few things straight before we get going. Hopefully, this chapter will give you the basic answers to some of the questions you're asked and then we can all hug it out and move on. Plus, if anyone sees you reading this book and starts with the grilling, you'll have some clear explanations to hand. Or, if all else fails, you can either suggest they buy a copy themselves or simply use your own to bash them over the head, before making a hasty run for it.

So, I've gathered together the most common questions I'm asked about shyness (both by non-shy people and shy people themselves), including some of the most controversial. Oh, and just for a laugh, I also trawled the internet for talk of all things shy, which has been eye-opening to say the least: Shy FX, Shy Carter, Shy Baldwin, Shy Glizzy . . . shy horses, bladders, bears and wolves. Who knew?

Question 1: 'What actually is shyness?'

I've been wading through a mountain of books and reports and articles about shyness, and it turns out, even scientists and psychologists don't agree on what it is.

Surprisingly, for something that is part of life for so many people, there isn't one clear definition of shyness. It's all a bit woolly and subjective, which may explain some of the confusion and aggro associated with it.

The best official definition that I've found is from the American Psychological Association:

Shyness is the tendency to feel awkward, worried or tense during social encounters, especially with unfamiliar people. Severely shy people may have physical symptoms like blushing, sweating, a pounding heart or upset stomach; negative feelings about themselves; worries about how others view them; and a tendency to withdraw from social interactions. Most people feel shy at least occasionally. Some people's shyness is so intense, however, that it can keep them from interacting with others even when they want or need to – leading to problems in relationships and at work.*

When faced with something or someone new or uncertain, shyness makes us feel awkward, uncomfortable or anxious. We fear judgement and criticism, even when there is none, and worry about falling short of the polished version of perfection we set for ourselves. And because we don't want to face these fears, we hide away. Shyness is a blend of self-consciousness, humility and reserve, all smooshed together. And it can cause us to bad-mouth ourselves for staying silent or for falling short. Shyness leads to so much negativity, sadness and shame. It can be all-encompassing.

Shyness is more than just a fleeting moment. It can occur before an interaction or situation, during it and for a long time afterwards too. It's the gift that keeps on giving.

Shyness is like a big resistance band holding us back. It elicits a strong urge to shrink and hide away, so that nobody can see or judge us. But, when we withdraw and live our lives in our shells, we miss out; on just about everything.

---

* Adapted from the Encyclopedia of Psychology: https://www.apa.org/topics/shyness

Question 2: 'What's the difference between shyness and social anxiety?'

The name 'social anxiety' scares me, because it seems like a huge label, compared with being shy. It sounds much more clinical.

Lee

Social anxiety is an extreme version of shyness. It's at the very far end of the shyness scale and it can dominate someone's life, stopping them from doing all kinds of daily activities, like going out with friends, eating in front of others or using public toilets. Social anxiety disorder (also known as SAD) can lead to things like depression, self-harm, drug issues and other not very nice stuff.

Social anxiety is not the same as shyness. It's a lot less common and it's a lot more debilitating. However, the term 'social anxiety' has become normalised, particularly on social media, and is being used more and more interchangeably with shyness. It's a hot topic, for sure, so I'll be donning my trench coat and we'll be investigating that further later on in the book.

Question 3: Are shy people anti-social?

It's a common misconception that shy people want to swerve social events because they're being anti-social. If staying home talking to the cat is your idea of a fun time, that's fantastic. In reality, however, we shy people long to have fun mucking around with other people; it's just that our fears and resistance are ripping up our social calendar; and not in a good way.

Before assuming that someone doesn't want to be part of the

conversation because they are being an arrogant arse, it might be worth considering that they are, in fact, a shy person, who really does want to be involved, but is struggling to join in.

Question 4: 'What's the opposite of shyness?'

Officially, the opposite of shyness is an outgoing personality. The words confident, loud, rowdy, unreserved, noisy, booming, flamboyant and strident also spring to mind. Outgoing people are open, friendly, chatty and gregarious. They love to be around other people, socialising and, erm, going out.

Question 5: 'How common is shyness?'

Shyness is more common than you might think. As I mentioned earlier, it seems that around 50 per cent of humans are shy, although results vary from survey to survey and the exact number changes depending on the country you're in, which really gets my inner geek going (so, I'll be delving into that in more detail later on too). Suffice to say, shyness is not rare, or uncommon or weird, and you are definitely not alone.

Question 6: 'Is shyness equally common in men and women?'

Shyness is often seen as a 'girly' trait, and I have to say, before I started exploring the shyness quagmire, I pretty much thought that too.

It turns out, though, that shyness affects both men and women. However, the way we view it is certainly gendered. While shyness in women can be seen as sweet and non-threatening, even a positive trait, men often have a hard time handling their shyness because they feel it impacts negatively on their masculinity and sex appeal. Searching the darkest depths of the internet to find out more, I discovered that, among some guys, shyness is the cause of much, erm, dissatisfaction. Eek.

> [Shyness is] by far, the worst possible trait for any male interested in any kind of intimate relationship with females. It is worse than incompetence, obnoxiousness, ugliness, and no sense of humor – combined.*

Blimey.

This is yet another reason why it's so important that we figure out a way to work with our shyness and stop it from being seen as a weakness. Then we can get on with hooking up, doing well at work and generally living our lives, without having to become lairy loudmouths.

Question 7: 'Is shyness the same as lacking confidence?'

I've always been quite shy. Very confident, but very shy.

Ruth Wilson, actor

Shyness and a lack of confidence are often seen as being one and the same. But when you think about it, they are actually quite separate.

It's perfectly possible to be confident in your abilities, but to feel shy about being seen, or heard.

---

* Shadowdemon, Urban Dictionary, 29 March 2005.

Let's imagine you're invited to go on a quiz show. You spend weeks swotting up on your chosen subject, reading every book and every article you can find. You know your stuff. You have facts swilling around your brain. We're talking expert level. So you're super-confident in your knowledge and in your ability to answer the questions correctly. If you were completing an online assessment, from the comfort of your bedroom, wearing furry slippers, you'd ace the test.

But the mere thought of speaking in front of an audience, being on camera, in the spotlight, and seen by millions of people, sends your levels of shyness sky high.

Shyness is the tendency to feel all kinds of awkward and self-conscious in new and uncertain situations – like being on TV! It's a fear of being seen and judged and is not a reflection of your confidence in your knowledge or abilities.

Question 8: 'What's the difference between shyness and introversion? Aren't they the same thing?'

I think people who are introverts are given more slack than us shy ones. Shyness is seen as something you need to 'get over', whereas if you are an introvert, then that's seen as just part of your personality.

Ben

I remember when I started planning this book, I asked this very question in an online group for introverts. Everyone got very offended. It was like I'd just chucked a grenade! I had to leave in the end. The vitriol was violent.

Being shy and being an introvert are not the same thing, although there is an overlap and they are often mixed up. Lots of shy people are also introverts. And some introverts are also shy. This is just my take on it. Please don't cancel me or send dog poo to my house.

Champion of introverts and author of *Quiet*, Susan Cain reckons shyness and introversion are like cousins. I like that. They're related and have some similarities, but they're not that close.

Introverts get their energy from being alone and from their inner world. When they've been around lots of people, they can feel over-stimulated and will need time to recharge and recover – for example, by hiding in a cupboard or making a swift exit. (Did you know that leaving a party without telling anyone is called a French Exit? Sounds kinda cool now, doesn't it?)

Introverts like spending time on their own because they enjoy their own company (not a euphemism) and are drained by being around people. Shy people may spend time alone, partly because they find it more com-fortable and partly because they are worried or awkward around others.

So, at a party, you may find shy people and introverts together in the kitchen helping with the washing up. But they are probably there for different reasons. And I think this is where the confusion arises. Introverts are elbow deep in dirty dishes because they are feeling drained; shy people are there because they're feeling awkward and uncomfortable around all these new people.

Either way, they are both in the kitchen. Doing the same damn thing. So, how about we are all a bit more understanding towards each other?

Introverts are portrayed as reading and studying and thinking a lot, so they're seen as intelligent and cool. Whereas shyness is viewed as a weakness.

Sinead

Shyness is seen as a weakness by many introverts, who don't connect with the concept of shyness at all. They are not anxious, or awkward, or afraid or uncomfortable. They feel strong and confident in their preferences. Which explains why some of them got all offended when I started talking about shyness.

I'm glad people are celebrating their introversion and owning it. It's lovely that there are sweatshirts and notebooks and pin badges galore adorning the introverts of the world.

So, how about we shy people start getting a bit more feisty? Let's do the same thing: stand up for ourselves and our shyness, rather than trying to hide it or apologise for it.

Question 9: 'Is there such a thing as a shy extrovert?'

Yes, there most certainly is. A shy extrovert is someone who likes socialising and gets their energy from being around others, but who also struggles with issues of fear and awkwardness. I am living proof that being shy and an extrovert is a thing.

The trouble with this gorgeous combination is that it can be fiercely frustrating. You want to be out there doing the things with the people, but you're battling resistance. It's like there's a barbed-wire fence in the way, and you're not up for shredding yourself to bits. And that's where the tension comes in. You're not really happy hiding away, being on your own and living a little life, but in order to have all the fun and enjoy all the possibilities, you have to find a way past your fears and insecurities.

Question 10: 'Is shyness a form of narcissism?'

Shyness has a strange element of narcissism, a belief that how we look, how we perform, is truly important to other people.

Andre Dubus, essayist

Right. I'm rolling up my sleeves here and flexing my fingers. I have to say, this is one of the most surprising accusations I've had to deal with.

Given that shy people are quiet and reserved, it seems counterintuitive to label us narcissistic. Surely spending so much energy worrying about what other people think of you makes you the opposite of self-obsessed?

According to Australian psychologist Paul Wink, there are two types of narcissism where the individual becomes fixated on their own needs.

The first is the more overt, extroverted kind of narcissism, where people are more likely to be cocky exhibitionists. Then there's the covert kind of narcissism, based on vulnerability which is linked to introversion, anxiety and defensiveness.

Hmmm. This makes me all kinds of uncomfortable. The last thing we shy people need is to have to deal with more negative vibes to wade through. And I have to admit, I was tempted to delete this section. However, the more I think about it, the more I can see how fixating on one's struggle, talking about it, thinking about it, mentioning it constantly, could perhaps become a form of self-obsession.

But my take on it is that I don't think it's helpful for us to be worrying about yet another thing that people may or may not think about us. After all, we need to get on with being mighty. So, if anyone mentions the link between narcissism and shyness to you, you could just thank them for their input, file their remarks away (in the bin) and move on.

Question 11: 'What's the shyest sign of the zodiac?'

Bit random, but, as I said, I'm answering your questions, and this is one I hear a lot. Virgo is reputedly the shyest astrological sign. Virgos are supposed to feel awkward, uncomfortable and nervous in new and unfamiliar situations. In true shy style, Virgos apparently don't just talk endlessly, they're more reserved and considered, and only say something when there's something to say. (I am pretty sure, though, that all shy people are not born between 23 August and 22 September. Although I did just miss that by a few days. Hmmm . . .)

Question 12: 'What is a shy bladder?'

Officially called paruresis, having a shy bladder is when you find it hard to pee when there are other people watching or in the room. It's like your pee is actually shy and can't perform under pressure. Apparently, it's really common. A simple way to sort it, though, in my humble opinion (based on no medical knowledge whatsoever), is to drink 2 litres of water a day, or maybe give birth to a very large baby; or, if you're looking for a more convenient (and less painful) solution, you could simply try closing and locking the bathroom door.

Question 13: 'Is shyness a weakness?'

I've seen shyness described as a disease, a prison, and even a disability. Harsh. Admittedly, it's not a whole load of fun. Being shy can be challenging. It can make life complicated. School and work and socialising are trickier. No doubt about it. It can feel like shyness is controlling you, dominating you and keeping you small.

But being shy doesn't mean you are broken, or weak or doomed to fail. Without wishing to sound glib, or twee, it seems to me that we have a choice: let it defeat us; or try to look for the positives in there. Embrace the things that make us us, and work with our shyness.

The fact that there are so many questions about shyness demonstrates how much work there is to be done to raise awareness and improve our understanding.

Knowledge is power, people!

SHY POINTS

- Shyness is the tendency to feel awkward or worried in uncertain or unfamiliar situations.
- Shyness affects people in different ways and in different situations, to different extents.
- Social anxiety is a very extreme form of shyness.
- Being outgoing is the opposite of shyness.
- Shyness is common! Around half of all people are shy.
- Shyness is equally common in men and women, although it can affect them differently.
- Shyness is not the same thing as lacking confidence.
- Shyness is related to, but not the same as, introversion.

CHAPTER 2

SHY BABY

Scientists have found the gene for shyness. They would have found it years ago, but it was hiding behind a couple of other genes.

Jonathan Katz, comedian

The traditional view of shyness is that something difficult or even traumatic must have happened to us to make us this way. But what if that's not the case? Is it possible that we can be born shy? I decided to investigate. And what better place to start than with a furry bundle of fluff?

Bobby the dog was only a few weeks old when I first met him. Although I'd had a dog when I was growing up, on that day part of me felt as anxious as if I was about to go and buy a baby. Clearly, I would never buy a baby, for so, so many reasons, but you know what I mean.

The velvety puppies were all in a big pen with their mum. A cacophony of Cavapoos. They were ridiculously cute, all scrambling around, playing, rolling and wiggling.

Standing there looking down at the puppies, I had the responsibility of choosing the newest member of our family. No pressure.

I considered the five furry bundles. And it was clear to me they were all different. A couple seemed quite wild. My husband and son had never had a dog before, so an out-of-control canine tearing around the place might be a bit too much for them. And then at the back of the pen, I spotted a rather round, rather reserved little ball of fluff. He seemed cautious, as though pondering whether to go see what all the fuss was about. I bent down to say hi to him and let him sniff me. And before I knew it, he was stuck to my legs, snuffling and shuffling along. I picked him up. He snuggled into the crook of my arm and fell asleep. A tiny furry baby limpet. My heart melted into a puddle on the floor. And that was it. I called the others and told them to come and meet our new doggie.

Bobby is five now, and he's exactly as he was then. He's quiet and cautious. When he plays with other dogs, he hangs out on the edge of the group, barking encouragement every now and again. He's not into wrestling, confrontations or loud noises. He's sensitive to stress and upset. If there's hormonal rage in the house (not mine, obviously), he gets upset and shakes. When I'm poorly, he sticks to me like glue and makes sure I'm ok. Bobs is a lover, not a fighter.

The reason I'm telling you all about Bobby is partly because I am a dog mum, so I can talk about him all day long. But also because his quiet nature is part of who he is. I'm convinced that Bobs was born shy. When I first met him, he was only a few weeks old. He hadn't left the house. He had only really hung out with his mum and his siblings. He hadn't suffered anything stressful or traumatic. He hadn't been forced to sing on stage or stand up in front of his class and read a poem. He is the way he is. And that's why we love him.

But rather than basing my theories on one fluffy dog, let's see what the experts make of this. And you'll be pleased to hear they've kept to the cuddly theme.

Scientists have investigated whether shyness is part of our personalities by observing cute, fuzzy kittens and tiny baby monkeys. They discovered that, from a very young age, around 15 per cent of the teeny, fluffy little critters were more hesitant and reserved. These shy baby monkeys and kittens were more likely to get stressed when separated from their mums and nervous when they met new people or animals. They concluded that, because the tiny fur balls were shy from such a young age, shyness was part of their fluffy genetic make-up. So, Bobs and I were right!*

But what about people? I guess it might make sense to look at actual humans too.

I think I was born shy, but I know being brought up to be good and quiet held me back too. My daughter isn't as shy, but scared of getting things wrong, even if I tell her not to worry.

Simon

According to scientists, we only become aware of ourselves as separate from other humans at around eighteen months old. That's when our sense of self is formed. And, because shyness is linked to feelings of self-consciousness and judgement, some people believe it cannot exist before that age. This school of thought would mean that babies cannot be shy.

And yet, if you've hung out with any babies lately, I'm sure you'll know that some are more nervous and freaked out by people they don't know than others. Some babies cry when held by strangers.

---

* J. Kagan, S. Reznick and N. Snidman, 'Biological Bases of Childhood Shyness', *Agricultural & Environmental Science Database*, 8 April 1988, p. 167.

Some seem to be more sensitive to new people and uncertain situations. Some are more reserved and quieter and less keen to be thrust into the arms of every passing old lady or launched into the air by random uncles.

I'm a twin. My brother, Ben, is ten whole very long minutes older than me. And no, before you ask, we are not identical. (I'm always amazed by the number of people who ask me that. Because the reason we are not identical is simple: he's a boy and I'm a girl, so we are not the same in a few fairly fundamental ways.) Anyway, he's a nice guy, my brother; very chilled and very brainy. He lives in Canada with his wife and three kids and is an outdoorsy chap who loves running, cycling and, for some reason I cannot fathom, camping. But why am I telling you about Ben? Well, as part of my research for this book, I underwent some hypnosis. And this is where things get a little strange. Honestly, this is so weird, I can't even believe I'm sharing it. It's not something I thought I would ever believe in or experience. But I've started to see what an incredible tool the brain is.

Under hypnosis, I visited the moment I was born. So, there I was, in my mum's tum, and my brother had just decided he'd had enough of being cooped up, and off he went. (He is an adventurer, after all.) In my memory, I sort of even waved him off. Byeeee! I was left on my own. And I thought to myself. Nah, I'm all good. I think I'll just stay here. It's nice. Maybe I was just glad to finally get some peace and quiet after all those months of being squished together with my brother.

Under hypnosis, I remembered the feeling of being alone and I liked it. I remembered the feeling of being safe and warm, where nobody could see me or reach me. And I liked that too.

Now, as you can imagine, my mum wasn't particularly keen on the idea of me spending another few months in there. Measuring four foot eleven, I think my mum was fed up with being wider than she was tall. The doctors were also apparently keen for me to come out. So, they sent for reinforcements and grabbed something closely resembling a toilet plunger, which they used to drag me out, kicking and screaming.

There was no reason for me to want to stay behind. In fact, you'd think I would want to stick with Ben, or at least follow him. There were literally no outside influences at this point. I didn't experience feelings of fear. I just wasn't that keen on coming out into the open. I liked the safe feeling of being hidden. Still do. So, while I admit that this is not a strictly scientific form of research, it would appear that even before I was born, I was shy. This experience and these memories make me think that I was shy from the get-go, and that shyness is an innate part of my personality.

The shy brain

My mum is quite shy and my dad quiet; I feel like shyness is part of my personality. I do feel like I was born like this, that it is my default position.

Sarah

Scientists have discovered evidence that points towards shyness being part of the way our brains are built.

Personality experts consider shyness to be connected to the 'threctic temperament', linked with a sensitive nervous system that is overly susceptible to threat and conflict.

Our brains have a kind of big red 'ALERT' button, which scientists call the behavioural-inhibition system. When something bad or scary is about to happen to us, our nervous systems raise the alarm. Everyone has an alert button, but some of us have a more finely tuned, more sensitive wiring system. Therefore, some of us are a lot more susceptible to scary things. We are more likely to want to give pain, punishment, fear and danger a very wide berth. Personally, I think that's a pretty smart way to be. But then me (and Bobby the dog) are biased in that direction.

Apparently, we shy people have a whole bunch of chemical things going on in our brains that make us this way. It's been suggested that our hypothalamus (a small region at the base of the brain) is more sensitive to new or scary or random changes and our amygdala is excitable!

Another theory is that we were born with more of the stress hormone norepinephrine zooming around our bodies. When our brains think something stressful has happened, the hormone floods our bodies, triggering blood flow and increasing our heart rate, making us more alert.

When we are scared of a new situation, with more of this norepinephrine stuff whizzing around, we would feel shyer more often than someone with less of it.

Let's talk vagal tone . . .

. . . and no, this is not a pelvic-floor exercise.

The vagus is one of the main nerves in our parasympathetic nervous system. It runs down the neck, across the chest and down to the tummy, signalling to the brain to tell it what's occurring in our organs, its main role being to calm said organs. The stronger a person's vagal tone, the better they are at calming down, slowing their breathing and heart rate and rebalancing and regulating blood glucose levels in a stressful situation. It's another bodily function that distinguishes wary from non-wary babies. Babies and kids with lower vagal tone are more likely to be shy.*

Scientists have also discovered that something called right frontal EEG asymmetries can determine fearfulness, cautiousness and behavioural inhibition in our personalities. These brain patterns can predict which tiny kid will become a shy bigger kid. They've shown that infants with more relative right frontal asymmetry are more likely to withdraw from mild stress, whereas infants with the opposite pattern of activation are more likely to approach scary stuff.†

Is shyness in our genes?

Like me, my mum and grandad have both had to conquer shyness, so perhaps there is some genetic tendency.

Aoife

It seems that shyness can be part of our physical make-up. It's a function of the way our brains are built. But is shyness in our DNA? Is it possible to inherit shyness from your parents, along with those sparkly eyes of yours?

In a 1996 study, Professor Cathy Mancini from McMaster University in Canada studied socially anxious parents and their kids, to see if the children had social anxiety too. She discovered that 49 per cent of the kids had some kind of anxiety disorder, a much higher rate than

---

* K. H. Rubin, in *International Encyclopedia of the Social & Behavioral Sciences*, 2001.
† K. H. Rubin, in *International Encyclopedia of the Social & Behavioral Sciences*, 2001.

average, which suggests that feeling socially anxious does get passed on from parent to child.*

> *Shyness is in my personality. I am sixty-seven now, but it took me until I was fifty to embrace how I actually am and not feel inferior because of it. My children are on the shy, retiring side, and one of my grandchildren shows this too. I want her to know she is great as she is.*
>
> Ann

I wondered if my shyness was inherited, or if I was an anomaly in my family. There were signs. My dad has been particularly interested in my Shy and Mighty project. I discovered one day, not from my dad, but from something my mum said, that my dad is shy. I'd had no idea. My dad is a super-successful professor. He's been on TV, he's met the Queen, written books, given talks all over the world. Surely he couldn't be shy?

So, did we have a conversation about it? Don't be daft. We're shy. I sent him an email, silly. Admittedly, he was pretty weirded out talking to me about this stuff, because it is personal. I promised I'd keep it confidential, apart from publishing it in my book. Oh, how we laughed.

Anyway, over to you, Dad:

> *I was probably born shy. I think that both my parents were shy. My dad worked out ways of dealing with it, but my mum never really did.*
>
> *A lot of my shyness experiences early on (and still, to some extent) relate to speaking up in a public forum. I can still find speaking*

---

* B. Markway and G. Markway, *Painfully Shy: How to Overcome Social Anxiety and Reclaim Your Life,* St Martin's Press, 2003, p. 34.

up difficult in any situation that feels competitive. 'Feels' is a key word. But I have learned how to deal with it by telling myself that I am good enough, that I have something interesting or valuable to contribute. And sometimes it even works.

When shyness happens, there's a feeling of trying to build up the strength to try and overcome it. And then annoyance – for example, because of a lost opportunity. It certainly affected my personal relationships when I was a kid and then a teenager. It did not really affect me at school in the classroom – if I feel very confident, then the shyness disappears. It affected me in my first job, and I then decided that I needed to deal with it. So, my second job was to become a lecturer which required me to teach and, to some extent, perform. This forced me to find ways to deal successfully with the problem.

Diversity is a good thing in any group human endeavour. Otherwise, we have groupthink, and a strong chance that decisions will not be optimal because not all possibilities will have been explored. It is easy for discussions to be dominated by the loudest, and it is important for any leader to ensure that all contributions are heard and considered.

Nadia's very cool dad, Steve

So, shyness runs in our family. And I'm glad it's out in the open; well, via email and a book, anyway.

Shyness is in our bodies and our brains and our genes. For many of us, it's always been there. From the moment that tiny ball of cells started growing into us. If our parents are shy, we're more likely to be shy too. And if we're born shy, we're more likely to grow into shy kids and then shy adults.

It breaks my heart because my son is shy as well. I am trying my best to make his childhood better than mine.

Azalia

Does that mean it's going to be part of us and our lives for ever? And should we just pull the blanket up over our heads, roll over on the sofa and order another extra-large pizza for one?

We should, of course, love ourselves the way we are.

But holding on to the label shy and hugging it close to our chests as we hide away from the world is not going to be a fun way to live.

We can move the dial. If we want to.

We can become stronger, braver and mightier. If we want to.

There is always room to work on ourselves and develop. It's about understanding our shyness and learning to work with it – not trying to change our personalities and swap them in for louder ones.

And that's why this book is not called Shy, but Shy and Mighty.

SHY POINTS

- There is evidence that shyness is hard-wired into our brain chemistry.
- Many shy people believe they were born shy.
- The nervous system in a shy person can be more sensitive to new, uncertain or scary things.
- Shyness can be in our DNA and can be inherited.

CHAPTER 3

SHY LIFE

In my quiet, I was working something out.

Keanu Reeves, actor

Everyone's experience of shyness is different. There's no one-size-fits-all shyness sweater, with very long, floppy sleeves and a big hood for us to hide under. Your shyness is different from mine. And I think that's why shy people can be confusing to others; we don't necessarily fit a cookie-cutter shape of a shy person.

Shyness is complicated. Oh, and let me just put this out there: you don't have to pass an exam and get a certificate authenticating you as a shy person – you're entitled to your feelings. Nobody can tell you otherwise. If you're shy, you're shy. No matter what anyone else says.

It's a funny thing that outgoing people often seem to feel that they can dismiss shyness, particularly if they don't think we fit their idea of what a shy person is. The last thing we need when experiencing shyness is someone telling us we're not really shy, or that we just need to get over it. They may have good intentions and simply want to help, or perhaps they're confused because we're not shy all the time or our shyness is not visible to them. Or it could be that they are uncomfortable dealing with other people's emotions and complexities. Or perhaps they just don't understand. Often, though, they are masking their own vulnerabilities and our shyness is triggering something within them.

But whatever the reason, when someone minimises or belittles our shyness, they're denying and dismissing our feelings. Crushing someone's feelings is not cool.

I am fighting a battle that no one knows about.

Charlie

Adding to the random patchwork nature of shyness, it can affect people in different ways. There are theories, academic arguments and sliding scales galore. It's like there's an entire spectrum of shyness spectrums. (Now that would be a fun diagram.) The most memorable is the Cheek and Buss shyness scale, which makes me think of butt cheeks on bus seats.

But here's what we really need to know.

Level 1: Kinda Shy

At the lowest end of the scale, shyness can simply mean that you're a quiet person. Perhaps you take a while to warm up around new people; perhaps you prefer hanging out on your own; or perhaps you'd rather steer well clear of doing certain things, such as going to raves and getting off your face with 60,000 other sweaty people. Seems like a smart move, to me. You might be a little uncomfortable in the company of new people until you warm up, get to know them and relax. Putting yourself out there, giving talks or standing on a stage could feel scary, but given the right kind of support and encouragement, you're able to do it. Like my first car, an old Rover Metro, you just need time to warm up. That's why, when you bump into someone new, engaging in small talk can feel excruciating. It also explains why you can be witty and relaxed with a group of friends you've known for years.

It does not affect my relationships because I feel comfortable around my partner and close friends. My close friends say they don't even realise I am shy, because I am outgoing around them.

Max

Level 2: Pretty Shy

Mid-level shyness happens more often and can be more limiting. You might feel embarrassed and self-conscious in a range of different situations and have a strong urge to avoid things that are new and uncomfortable. Common circumstances that trigger shyness may include standing on a stage, presenting your work to a group of people, talking to important people or people in a position of authority, meeting clients, ordering food in a restaurant, standing up for yourself in a discussion, putting your hand up in class, meeting someone new, talking to someone you want to snog the face off.

You might find it hard to express your needs, to disagree with someone or to have a difficult conversation. You miss out on social events and seeing friends and on dating opportunities. You don't share your ideas and opinions. You keep your achievements to yourself. You stand back and let other people get the credit you deserve. You avoid saying what needs to be said. You hide. You bottle it all up.

You become an expert at avoiding stuff you don't like. Personally, I'm not a fan of phone calls. I hate phoning people I don't know and

I hardly ever leave voice messages. In fact, if you ever get one from me, you'll know that you've made it to my inner circle.

And because you need time to warm up, it can take you a little longer to do things, like making friends, settling down, finding your dream job, or getting promoted at work. You get there in the end, but in the moment, feeling like you're lagging behind is frustrating.*

You're not big into sharing your feelings. No surprise there. You're shy! And there's a lot of embarrassment and shame swirling around too, so you definitely don't talk about shyness.

What do you do instead? You keep all your fears and worries locked away. That way, they can really build up and fester, leading to even more unhappiness and anxiety. Boom. Now, I'm no psychologist, but I'm pretty sure that's not very good for anyone's mental or physical wellbeing.

It could also be the case that people around you might not have a clue that you've got all kinds of shy thoughts going on. You might feel like you can give talks or sing on stage, but it's all a bit of an act – because if you were to stop pretending or masking your emotions, you would feel shy and awkward, and have an overwhelming urge to hide.

Level 3: Very Shy

And then, at the more extreme end of the spectrum, some shy people may feel shy all the time, every single day. For them, shyness feels like it's part of their personality; it's part of who they are, on a deep level.

Really severe shyness is more debilitating and is sometimes called

---

* A. Caspi, G.H. Elder and D.J. Bern, 'Moving Away From the World: Life-course Patterns of Shy Children', *Developmental Psychology*, vol. 24 (1988), pp. 824–831.

social anxiety, as mentioned earlier. You may feel like you've been shy your whole life, and you feel like you're shy pretty much all day every day, in all situations. You might feel like shyness is part of you and that you'll never not be shy. Severe shyness has a huge impact – professionally and personally – and can cause you to feel incredibly isolated.

No matter how shy you feel, no one level of shyness is more important than another. We are all in this together.

When are we shy?

If shyness is a reaction to newness and uncertainty, it's hardly surprising that we feel more shy in some situations than others. We're a lot less likely to feel shy when we're all safe and snug watching telly with the dog than if we're shoved onto the stage at an open mic night at the local comedy club.

We feel particularly shy in busy social situations, such as parties and networking events. We hug the walls (I guess that's why we're sometimes called wallflowers) or hide in the loo.

We struggle with small talk, which is why when we bump into someone in the street we get a strong urge to dive into the nearest bush, or shop, or passing car.

We don't like being the centre of attention or having people look at us. The prospect of having people sing 'Happy Birthday' to us in a busy restaurant, complete with mariachi band, is tantamount to torture.

We find it hard to speak up in meetings or group discussions, particularly if we feel a lack of authority or power in relation to others. We'd rather slide off the chair than speak up and share our ideas. The discomfort of putting ourselves on the line, with all eyes on us, feels too much to handle.

It's common to feel shy around strangers, people who we are physically attracted to, and people in authority. So, attempting to chat to a hot firefighter we've just laid eyes on is going to be particularly difficult.

And because shyness is often a reaction to newness, it may seem to ebb and flow at different times in our lives. For example, starting a shiny new job, moving to a new town, getting back on the dating scene after a break-up, or feeling self-conscious having put on a few pounds, may all exacerbate shyness. But once we get used to our new situation, our shyness fades and we feel more comfortable.

How does shyness make us feel?

When shyness happens, we are flooded with feelings. Worries and fears and doubts are unleashed inside us and start to bombard our brains.

> *I feel like everyone is looking at me, that I am saying something stupid, that everyone thinks I am stupid.*
>
> Roisin

The doubts. And negative thoughts. They take over. We worry that people are judging us, that we won't be good enough, that we'll mess up, that people might laugh at us. We feel uncomfortable and awkward and self-conscious. We feel nervous, jittery, on edge and embarrassed.

> *They're not interested in that, shush. Let them talk; you'll sound stupid. Wait until there is a gap in the conversation . . . now . . . no, now . . . no . . . wait.*
>
> Elodie

We catastrophise. We imagine the worst and pick over the past. We examine every little thing that happened and look for clues to justify all our negative feelings. We build the future up into a big fiery ball of flames and fear, giving ourselves even more excuses to hide away.

Shyness makes us want to hide, or run away, to escape the situation we are in. It feels like we're digging our heels in and being dragged towards a fate worse than total humiliation. Given the choice, we would lurk our way through life, totally unnoticed.

In my head, it's a big rant about how inadequate I am, how I'll never be able to do what I want to do and how odd and boring everyone must think I am. And stupid – because I can't seem to speak quickly enough, say smart things or make funny jokes.

Laura

The heavy blanket you're wearing is holding you back. Deep down, you may actually want to become a magician, a burlesque dancer, a rapper or an inspirational speaker. You may want to share your ideas at work, stand up for your opinions, make some friends, be part of the gang, and chat with that person over there standing by the bar. I mean, it's not a lot to ask, right?

But you can't.

So you miss out.

It's annoying. And upsetting. And frustrating. The fact that we can't do the things we want to do can make us feel pretty pissed off. We can feel excluded, isolated and rejected.

And that's why I'm writing this book.

How does shyness affect us physically?

When we feel shy, all the negative thoughts and fears and feelings that are swirling around our brains affect us physically as well.

> *I feel my face getting red and I have to avoid eye contact. In extreme situations, like public speaking, I start shaking, hyperventilating and sometimes people say I look like I'm about to cry.*
>
> Odette

Our brains trigger a stress reaction and pump out a shock wave of cortisol, prompting the classic fight-or-freeze response. We are on 'shy alert' and our bodies take over: we blush, we flush, our hearts pound, our breath quickens. We might feel faint or even have a panic attack. We tense up, our chests tighten, our breathing becomes jagged, we feel nervous, panicky and jangly, teary and edgy. We get a swimmy tummy, need a panic wee – and even feel like we will actually poop our pants or throw up. Eugh.

We get boiling hot, clammy and sweaty in funny places. We hunch, we avoid eye contact and suddenly find the floor very interesting. We feel frozen and, like a cartoon rabbit in the headlights, we go wobbly and start shaking and quaking. Faced with our fears, blood rushes away from our brains towards our feet, in an attempt to help us run for it, making us feel dizzy or headachey. We feel frozen to the spot.

> *An overwhelming bout of shyness can affect me at any time, but larger social events and speaking to more than two or three people at a time can panic me. I feel nauseous or lightheaded and I've had numerous occasions when IBS has kicked in. As I've got older (I'm*

fifty-one), I've learned to control my breathing, in and out from my
nose, which helps.

Pauline

Our minds go blank and our tongues get tied up, our throats tighten,
our mouths go dry and our speech goes shaky or slurry. And because
we can't get the words out, it plays into our fears of being judged. How
can we make a sensible point in a meeting when we're stumbling over
our words and sweating through our shirts? We panic *because* we're
panicking – focusing on the fact that we're shaking and blushing and
on what to do about it, leaving not much brain space to get on with
the job in hand. Our brains spiral into a shyness vortex.

Oh, it's a joy!

How does shyness affect our behaviour?

Shyness stops me from putting my own dreams into practice.

Gilly

When we're in the darkest depths of shyness, experiencing all those
negative feelings and physical reactions has an impact on the way we
behave, the things we do and the way we live our lives.

I'd love to get a master's degree, but I fear group discussions. I love
playing music, but I get stage fright. I love writing, but fail to see
how I would get anywhere with it if I'm too shy to share my work.
Life is limiting and disappointing because of my shyness.

Imani

Faced with all this difficult stuff, we choose comfort and safety. We put our comfort blankets over our heads and we hide – from new, uncertain and challenging situations, from putting ourselves out there, from speaking up and showing up. From life.

Being shy at school

I was so scared and so shy back then. I mean, I grew up in one of the biggest high schools in the world, and that's the Disney Channel. Everybody was falling in love with each other or not liking each other, and it was exhausting, and I was the shy one in the corner.

Selena Gomez, singer*

The hiding starts early. And so does the missing out. The hubub and chaos of loud, noisy classrooms favour loud, noisy kids. Shy kids struggle to speak up and be heard.

In class, shy kids may know the answers but never say so. They avoid sharing their work and their ideas. They avoid standing up in front of the class, getting involved in activities and teams, performing under pressure, competing. They worry about putting up their hands in case they make a mistake. They don't like being put on the spot, being looked at or having to speak in front of lots of people.

School is the worst place to be shy. Any assignments that involve standing up and talking – they all scared the absolute shit out of me. I struggled to make friends, and even though I now have a close

---

* https://www.bustle.com/articles/151022-14-celebs-who-are-shy-from-kanye-west-yes-really-to-kristen-stewart

circle of people that understand me, it's still annoying to not feel comfortable speaking up in a group.

Sam

I remember sitting in a class discussion. I had a lot of ideas and things I wanted to say. Until the teacher said those fateful words, 'We'll go round the room,' and pointed to the guy on his left. I was sitting to his right. My heart sank. I was going to be last. I'd have to wait. And come up with something new, that nobody else had said. My heart started beating faster and I felt a sudden urge to run away. But I was trapped with my back against a bookcase and couldn't move an inch. There was nowhere to run. By the time it was my turn, my voice was so tiny, barely anything came out. It was twenty-five years ago, yet I remember the panic so clearly.

Shy children avoid big groups, parties, sleepovers, invitations, opportunities and new experiences that make them feel uncomfortable or scared or worried. They are often found on the edge, watching from a distance, feeling like they don't fit in.

I used to love trampolining and there was a club in school. I went for a day and I felt so uncomfortable and anxious because no one from my year was there. They stared at me for being the youngest. I ended up quitting.

Lynn

Our school experience is meant to set us up for life. Sadly, these formative years can also leave us scared, and scarred, for life.

Shy kids may not know why they feel the way they do. As a result, they may come across as stubborn or difficult, facing frustration and irritation from parents and teachers alike.

But shy children are not being deliberately obstructive. A kid who stops speaking at school is not doing it to annoy the teacher or to be defiant. It could be that they feel so anxious that the words won't come out. It could be that the whole school experience is simply too overwhelming, too noisy and too intimidating for them to feel comfortable. And without the right kind of support and encouragement, they will continue to shrink.

How do shy people socialise?

I saw a friend in a supermarket and ran away!

Jae

Take one very large room, some very loud music, a whole herd of extroverts, outrageous dancing, endless alcohol and mix it together with a shedload of insecurities. And what do you have? A shit storm of shyness, that's what.

I'd got all dressed up for the party, but now that I was there, all I wanted to do was go home. All my friends were on the dance floor, but I knew I would need a few more drinks before I could even contemplate dancing, let alone relax enough to actually enjoy it.

While everyone else seemed to be having fun, I was propping up the bar, wishing I could join in, but knowing that I couldn't, feeling so self-conscious.

That sounds self-obsessed, doesn't it? I knew nobody was looking at me. They were too busy doing slut drops and downing shots to care. But I just could not shift the feeling that I was trapped under a blanket of shyness. Instead of joining in, I stood there like a muppet, on my own, wondering when I could go home.

It was painful. And not very much fun.

When you're a shy person, socialising with other humans can be uncomfortable in the extreme.

We find it hard to relax. It seems like everyone is having way more fun. The chances of us dancing on the tables, or on the floor for that matter, are slim. We are neither the life nor the soul.

Rather than getting locked up for partying too hard, we choose to get locked inside our own head. We worry about looking bad, about saying the wrong thing, about making a fool of ourselves. We are so busy worrying that we forget to have a good time.

We find small talk totes awks. Attempting to slide smoothly into a conversation is more sick than slick. Chatting in a chilled-out fashion with groups of people makes us hot, and not in a good way. We find it hard to get a word in. And if we do manage to say something, being heard is hard.

Recently, at a dinner party, a friend attempted to invite me into the conversation, by asking me about my work. Before I could finish my sentence, I was interrupted by a rather loud woman, who is a teacher. She started explaining shyness to us all because she'd picked up a book about introverts. I tried to rejoin the conversation and bring it back to my friend's initial question. I felt belittled and irritated. No matter how hard I tried, I just couldn't seem to make myself heard. In the end I stopped trying and buried my head in a large glass of wine.

Given I'm a shyness expert, and I've written two books on the subject, isn't it ironic that my shyness is what holds me back from talking about my work. I can see the funny side, but that experience irked me. I'm annoyed with myself for being silenced and for choosing to spend my time in the company of people who clearly don't care about me or what I have to say.

How do we get on with getting it on?

I missed out on dating a guy who seemed really cool. Shyness crept up on me and resulted in me freezing up, avoiding eye contact and essentially ignoring him whenever he was around. He was paying me attention, staring at me and hinting he wanted to chat. I just couldn't risk saying something unintelligent. So I said nothing at all.

Ali

Romantic relationships can be tricky for shy people. We struggle to approach people we don't know in the first place, and it's hard to show your best side when you're a sweaty betty who can't seem to string a sentence together. For us, flirting is fraught with fear and awkwardness. And it can take time to warm up. Once we are in a relationship, we can also struggle with sex, and we may have difficulty expressing our needs or having open discussions.

The sad thing is that being in a relationship helps us to feel safe, secure and supported. We feel less lonely and self-conscious when we are with someone who loves and believes in us. We feel happier.

Yet, when we hide, we miss out on love.

I found it very difficult to form a stable relationship with a long-term partner. I haven't had kids because I didn't feel confident about having to bring them up assertively.

Megan

It's not that we don't want to date and do the do with other people – because we do. It's just that navigating this stuff is hard.

When my son, Jacob, was a baby, I started to worry about whether I had it in me to be a parent. Talk about trying to close the stable door after the horse has bolted! How can I be a mum when I'm so bad at being boss? It's one thing to push a babbling baby around in a buggy, but how to tame a rogue toddler, or discipline a greasy, wayward teenager?

Erm.

I've been muddling through. Clearly, I don't know what I'm doing. And there are so many times when I mess up.

Here's the thing. There isn't one way to parent. I can't seem to do strict, or authoritarian. But, I can do approachable and empathic.

No parents are perfect. (Lucky for me.) Rather than holding ourselves to such high standards, what if having kids gave us the purpose and motivation we need to be more mighty? I know I don't want my kid to see me hide away from making phone calls or having difficult conversations. I want him to see me being awesome!

How does shyness impact our career prospects?

All this hiding has an impact on our professional prospects too. Research shows that outgoing people are more likely to get promoted, earn more money and work in senior positions than shy people.

I've had panic attacks caused by shyness during interviews, which have resulted in my not getting jobs. I come across as too nervous and shy, unable to communicate properly. It's led me to retreat to a self-employed career, which has dented my confidence and hampered my prospects.

Richard

We avoid speaking up in meetings and are often completely silent. We are told to contribute more but finding your voice in an environment dominated by extroverts can feel impossible.

The longer you remain silent at work, the longer you keep your ideas and opinions locked away, the harder it becomes to speak up and contribute. Getting stuck in a rut of silence, makes hitting our unmute button feel like a dramatic event. The less often you speak, the more likely it is that all eyes will be on you when you do.

It's not just talking in front of people we don't know that intimidates us. We are also daunted by people in authority, people we feel are in competition with us and people we know well. Even if they don't mean to, knowing that everyone in the room is rooting for you can feel like a lot of pressure!

> *I find talking in front of people I don't know difficult. Even talking on Zoom gives me anxiety. I don't feel the working world is geared towards shy people.*
>
> Fliss

Representing your work and your ideas can feel daunting, and the fear of judgement paralysing.

> *Although my job was mainly organisational, there were opportunities to speak in public. I should have grabbed these opportunities. I could have used the job to benefit my own career. But instead, I deliberately avoided them. I think my reticence to place myself in the spotlight meant that I ended up scrambling to find my next job.*
>
> Liev

We find it hard to put ourselves forward for opportunities. We avoid asking for pay rises. We tend to focus on doing the work, rather than talking up the fact that we've done it. We keep our heads down and get on with it.

We are so afraid of attracting too much attention, whether that's by messing up, or shining too brightly, that we can end up shuffling along, failing to fulfil our potential. We find it hard to play the game, to raise our profile and stand out, particularly in an environment that can feel cutthroat and competitive. So, we aim low, and go for jobs we know we can handle, ones that don't push us too much or force us to face our fears.

But when we fail to speak up, our potential is silenced. We are overlooked, underestimated, undervalued, underappreciated. We miss out, on recognition, success – and money!

I have been in touching distance of dream galleries, collaborators or customers and my shyness has led to keeping quiet and missing out.

Kath

There's a cost to shyness. It's hard to throw your hands in the air like you just don't care or live la vida loca when you're wearing a woolly blanket. And it's pretty tricky to give a serious work presentation and showcase your genius when you are dragging this scraggy thing around with you.

My shyness and the anxieties that come with it have infiltrated every aspect of my life at one time or another. I haven't spoken up at work when I have had good ideas, haven't gone for projects or commissions or jobs for fear of making a fool of myself. Far too often, I have accepted, when I should have said no, or stood back when I should have pushed myself forward.

Aylah

When our fears and limiting beliefs become stronger than our desire to move forwards, we can only watch and stare as recognition, prizes, fun, dates, love, relationships, jobs, promotions, pay rises slip away into the sunset.

The thing with wearing the blanket is that it's a choice. And it does serve a purpose: it protects us and keeps us safe and warm and snug; when we wear it, we don't take risks, and nothing much can hurt us. But keeping the blanket with us, means not living our lives to the full.

Maybe it's time to let the blanket go.

SHY POINTS

- Everyone's experience of shyness is different.
- Shyness is a reaction to new and uncertain situations.
- Shyness starts with a range of negative feelings.
- It also causes a physical reaction in our bodies.
- Shyness makes us hide away.
- We miss out in school, socially, in relationships, and at work too.
- When we hide, we miss out on living our lives.

CHAPTER 4

SHY SOCIETY

I was really shy, like, to the point where my parents would go to counsellor meetings for shy girls to try to get me out of it. I didn't like to be in front of people, so I would just watch.

Zendaya, actor*

'You're playing small. You're holding us back. It's pathetic!' she said.

I couldn't believe what I was hearing. Sneering, scornful derision from a colleague – someone who was supposed to be working with me, on my side, growing a business with me.

The aggression in her voice was ugly. I could picture her eyes bulging, veins throbbing, spit flying through the air, even over the phone.

My head was spinning. What was happening here? Where had this even come from? I knew we were different. She was the outgoing, ballsy one. The one who signed the deals and dealt with the tricky clients. I was the calm, quiet ideas person, the one our clients could trust. I

---

* https://www.bustle.com/articles/151022-14-celebs-who-are-shy-from-kanye-west-yes-re-ally-to-kristen-stewart

was the one who delivered on the – sometimes outlandish – promises she made.

I was pacing up and down my kitchen in my pyjamas and slippers, palms sweating as I listened to this tirade. My heart was smashing through my chest. I could feel everything I'd worked for come crumbling down around me. My ear, pressed hard against the phone, burned. It felt like the handset was about to spontaneously combust and blow my eyebrows clean off.

And then the clincher.

'Nobody takes you seriously. You're a joke.'

Bam. A sharp left hook to the cheekbone.

'You don't deserve to get paid the same as me.'

I felt a molten volcano of rage rise up within me. The worm was turning. (That made me the worm; not ideal, but for now it would have to do.)

This wasn't happening to me. Absolutely not. Not after all the hard work I'd put in.

I cleared my throat, took a breath and, in a steely voice I didn't recognise, said, 'It's over. You can expect to hear from my lawyer.'

Admittedly, that comeback kicked off six months of mayhem and stress – and a legal wrangle worthy of its own box set. But it certainly felt good to say. For that split second, I stood tall, slippers replaced with virtual heels, a sharp suit, pointy shoulder pads and bouffy hair. In your face, bitch.

I put down the phone, hands shaking, and started to cry. This wasn't the plan. In fact, it was so far removed from the plan, I may as well have been lost in a forest without a sat nav, or even a map, car dead, phone battery dead, with only a creepy hitchhiker with murderous intentions for company.

What if there really was something wrong with me? What if my shyness meant I was abnormal? I felt like a freak. A broken freak.

And very, very alone.

As I tried to recover from that harrowing experience, self-medicating with many, many gallons of ice cream, I began to think about what was going on in my head.

Why did I feel a strong sense of resistance when it came to speaking up or being seen? Why did I prefer to stay in the background, doing, making and writing things, rather than being centre stage? Why did I feel unable to big myself up or sell myself? My inhibitions had controlled my everyday life and my professional prospects for years, but I had never given them a voice, let alone questioned them or figured out how to work with them.

Instead, I struggled on, trying to be something I wasn't, and feeling like I never quite fitted in or made the grade. Imagine spending your life wearing shoes that are too small. I looked outside myself and tried to be more like other people; louder, more strident, more self-assured, more brazen. But all the while I felt freakish. I was convinced my reserved nature meant there was something wrong with me.

You're not alone

Let's get statistical. Brace yourself. In the 1970s, an influential and ground-breaking study on shyness was carried out in the USA by psychologists Philip Zimbardo, Paul Pilkonis and Robert Norwood. They found that 40 per cent of respondents labelled themselves as currently shy, 82 per cent said they had been shy at some point in their lives and a quarter said they'd been shy most of their lives. Only 18 per cent said they'd never labelled themselves as shy, and only 1 per cent said they'd never experienced shyness.*

Shyness varies from country to country. It seems that there's more shyness in Eastern and Asian cultures, with over 50 per cent reported. For example, 57 per cent of people in Japan and approximately 55 per cent in Taiwan consider themselves shy. Whereas most Western cultures – like Canada, Germany, India and Mexico – are in line with the USA and have around 40 per cent reported shyness.†

And, in Britain, 57 per cent of people describe themselves as shy. As a British shy person, it's comforting and empowering to know that, although I often feel weird and like I don't fit in, I'm actually part of the shy majority.‡

Wherever you live in the world, a big ol' chunk of us are shy. Shyness is not weird, or strange. It's normal.

So, where are all the shy people?

I thought, well, if I had the nerve, I'd be a singer. But I was always shy. And I always had this ambivalent feeling of wanting to be in the spotlight but being too shy to be in the spotlight.

Carly Simon, singer

---

* Philip Zimbardo, Paul Pilkonis, Robert Norwood, 'The Silent Prison of Shyness', Department of Psychology, Stanford University, 11 November 1977.

† B.J. Carducci, 'Cross-Cultural Comparisons of Shyness', in *Encyclopedia of Mental Health* (second edition), 2016.

‡ The YouGov Personality Study, 11 November 2019, https://yougov.co.uk/topics/lifestyle/articles-reports/2019/11/12/yougov-personality-studypart-one-British-reserve

Shyness can be a lonely and isolating experience. But given that half of us are shy, why is it that we feel so alone?

I will happily talk about being introvert, which I see as a way of thinking, but shyness is embarrassing. It feels childish, like something you should grow out of.

Andy

Being shy is fraught with anxiety, shame and embarrassment. These emotions mean we don't want to share our experience of being shy with others. It can feel like another stick to beat ourselves up with.

It's more accepted to talk about being an introvert. But that's frustrating because I'm not an introvert. I crave and am energised by connection. It's 'cool' to be an introvert these days; but talking about shyness seems taboo.

Sarah

When we feel shy, we withdraw into the background of our lives. Our struggle is silent. All the negative self-talk, catastrophising and self-consciousness and awkwardness happen in our heads. Our physical symptoms are mostly invisible.

We don't show up or speak up. And because we're not being seen or heard, our voices are missing from the conversation. That means other shy people don't see us either. And that only serves to exacerbate the sense of isolation we feel.

Being shy is not really a hot topic of conversation. When was the last time you told anyone you were feeling shy? Hmm. Me neither. I'm not sure I even admitted it to myself until I started this project.

It's not like showing off your latest tattoo, is it? It's more of an embarrassing rash.

I don't talk about my shyness. I don't think I've ever talked about it. It feels shameful.

Rosie

The fact that we shy people are quiet, and not keen on shouting about our feelings – or about anything, for that matter – makes us a hell of a lot less likely to want to talk openly about our shyness.

There's a cycle going on here. A vicious shy-cycle:

ANXIOUS FEELINGS > NEGATIVE SELF-TALK > HIDE > ISOLATION

And round and round we go.

Hoodwinked

I was a very, very shy child, and acting was an escape for me. I think a lot of actors say that. At the time, I was much more comfortable pretending to be other people than being myself. Acting really helped me get out of my shell. I wouldn't necessarily call myself shy now, but it was a real problem for me as a child.

Kate Mara, actor*

We like to blend into the background, wearing an invisibility cloak. And what would look good with that cloak? Ooh, I know. A mask.

---

* Booth Moore, *Los Angeles Times*, 19 June 2014.

When I'm at work, I'm in uniform. This is my suit of armour. I feel confident: I know my job, I don't put up with rude patients, I keep them laughing and make them feel cared about. I'm the person I'd like to be all the time. I'm not her, though. I find it exhausting being the quick-witted, bouncy nurse. But it's who the patients need.

Michelle

Because we're ashamed of our shyness, we conceal it. We cover up who we really are by putting on an act and pretending to be something we are not. We worry that revealing the real us will make us unlovable and repellent, so we wear a mask to protect us from failure and rejection and keep ourselves safe from judgement.

And there's a whole wardrobe of mask options. Whether you're after something sparkly with a hint of humour; a shiny, sarcastic disguise; or a sharp, pointy mask with an acerbic edge – there's bound to be something to suit you.

Our mask selection could be a conscious attempt to trick people into thinking we are more confident and outgoing than we really are. Or we may be masking our shyness subconsciously and not even know we're doing it.

Like the time in my first proper job when my HR director told me I used humour as a defence mechanism. For what? Silly. I batted him away. And made a joke about it. I was young. I had no real clue what he was on about.

But now, literally, right now as I'm writing this, I can finally see that I did use humour to mask my shyness. Making people laugh is easier than being honest about my self-consciousness and insecurities. Turns out my mask choice is a witty little number – so subtle, I had no idea I was wearing it.

I laugh a lot. To ease possible tension, to make things seem light-hearted, to fill awkward moments. The more nervous I am, the more I laugh. I'm talking nervous laughter, not real laughter.

Fiona

Sometimes, on a night out, I have been known to select an ice mask. Rather than getting involved in the dancing or, god forbid, karaoke, I'll lean on the bar, exuding cool indifference (pah!) and doing my best to look like I'm chilling out and just taking in the vibes, man. I do realise that this mask is the least likely to stay in place, or rather it's the most likely to melt off and end up in a puddle on the floor. And that's the thing with masks: they're not always believable.

But if you are partial to a mask, why not take it to the next level and become a professional?

People are usually surprised I'm shy. They just think I'm quiet. I've done lots of TV and radio interviews, given presentations and taken part in panels at big conferences. I actually don't mind it that much. I'm playing the part of being the voice of my organisation.

Clare

There are so many shy people masquerading as confident performers in theatre, cinema and on TV. Acting is basically being paid to wear a mask. If you struggle to be yourself, what better way to earn a living than to act? Sure, you'll have to find a way to actually get on the stage or in front of the camera without sweating buckets, throwing up or having a panic attack, but once you're there, it's way easier to pretend to be someone else than to be your true shy self.

People assume you can't be shy and be on television. They're wrong.

Diane Sawyer, newsreader

But, putting on an act just to get through the day is exhausting. Despite what we're told about faking it to make it, wearing a mask all day is not good for you. It's not good for your mental health and it makes it hard to connect with people.

There's no need for us to feel ashamed, or like we don't fit in. Instead of sinking into the background, let's be a bit more open about our shyness and be true to who we are. If people are proud to be sensitive, or proud to be introverted, why shouldn't we be proud to be shy?

Shyness pandemic

In 2020, as Covid-19 swept the globe, we lost so much, and life changed dramatically. Every now and again I'm struck by the craziness of it all; how for that period, life shrank to the size of our four walls and patch of garden, all squashed together, missing school and work and mingling and hugs.

I am not used to being in group situations like meetings or courses. This is where I get shy. I have not spoken in a large group for over a year and a half and the thought of being in that situation makes me sick.

Alex

We replaced the commute with a shuffle downstairs in slippers, swapped water-cooler chats for dog walks and podcasts. Instead of working the room, we wore masks and queued outside supermarkets, with 2 metres between us and the next person. Physical contact and connection were dangerous and scary. A matter of life and death. Many of us hardly left the house in months. It was a monk-like existence.

And wearing a mask became the norm.

In some ways, I liked wearing a mask, because I could hide behind it. I liked the fact that I could avoid bumping into people on the street and having to engage in small talk because nobody knew who I was. The trouble was, my already quiet voice was now completely muffled, and nobody could hear a word I was saying. I ended up having to repeat myself at least three times. It was excruciating.

The pandemic turned us into a society of paranoids. As police patrolled the streets and parks looking for rule-breakers and people started reporting their neighbours for breaches of social distancing, we felt judged by others. It was like something out of a sinister film, and a climate of fear descended upon us.

According to research, it takes anywhere from two to eight months to form a habit. Spending a year and a half in and out of lockdown led to our socially anxious tendencies being ramped up and embedded. After months of isolation, we became so used to being alone or safely wrapped up at home that being plunged back into real-life social situations felt decidedly unappealing to many. Our social skills rusted away to nothing. Even people who weren't shy before started to experience social anxiety.

Because I haven't had as much practice at socialising, I've gotten worse at it. I went to the supermarket, and it was one of the most terrifying experiences of my life. The lights were too bright, I felt like I was getting in the way of everyone, it felt like everyone was staring at me.

Rachel

Changes in society and the way we communicate are having an impact on our social skills, and that has a knock-on effect on our shyness.

I think I'm slowly increasing in shyness. I had spent the past two years working hard at my social skills and had plans to take things up a notch this year. The pandemic made me want to curl up into a ball and avoid all communication. I was frustrated at going back to square one with my shyness.

Habab

SHY POINTS

- We mask our shyness.
- Sometimes we try to self-medicate.
- We get stuck in a vicious cycle of feeling anxious, negative self-talk, hiding and isolation.
- When we mask our shyness, we end up feeling exhausted and disconnected from ourselves and others.
- The pandemic isolated us and increased our levels of shyness and social anxiety.

CHAPTER 5

SHY TECH

Quiet is the new loud.

Joe Robitail, writer

I have a hunch. I can feel it in my bones. It feels to me that shyness is on the increase; that there's a shy tide coming our way. Maybe, just maybe, the meek really will inherit the earth?

The WiFi Life

It seems to me that modern life and the way we use technology are making us more shy.

It's surprising how easy it is to never leave the house. If you wanted to become a recluse, you totally could. You wouldn't need to live in a forest in a hut made out of sticks and bits of mud. You'd just need WiFi.

While I was in isolation, due to Covid-19, I realised just how easy it is.

From the safety of my little front room, and thanks to super-speedy broadband, I was able to catch up on the news, watch TV, listen to the radio, do a little bit of exercise, message my clients and friends across a dizzying array of platforms, read books and magazines and spend way too many hours perusing shops and buying clothes and shoes and lots of pointless things. My brain was buzzing with interactions, but I'd realise that I'd not actually spoken for hours. All day. And you know? I didn't mind it one bit.

There was a legendary moment, when, craving the comfort of a hot chai (or shy) latte from Starbucks, I ordered an Uber Eats and had one delivered. (I realise this makes me a bad person on many levels, but they are so yummy.) With the touch of a button, someone brought me a hot drink. I didn't even need to open my mouth. Well, I did to drink it, but not to order it. There was no awkwardness. No human interaction whatsoever. No nothing. Apart from the shame of knowing that some kid on a bike was bringing me a hot drink, which seems so overly indulgent, it's ridiculous. But once I let go of the guilt, it was amazing. A shy person's paradise.

Shy tech

'Alexa, what's 244 x 13?' I hear my friend's son doing his homework. He's cheating, asking the virtual assistant robot thingy to do the work for him. At first, I'm horrified. But then I chuckle to myself; that cheeky little monkey.

I'm not a big fan of Alexa. She creeps me out and I'm pretty sure she's listening in on all our conversations, or maybe even tapping into our brain function. Have you ever had a thought, like, Oooh, I really fancy a pair of red sneakers, only to find that you're suddenly being stalked relentlessly by ads for red sneakers?

But I can't deny how handy these personal robot thingies are for us shy people. With a robot friend, we can avoid all kinds of conversations.

From finding online bargains and getting weather and traffic updates to discovering fitness tips, new music and the latest news or sports updates. We can book appointments, give to charity and even send virtual hugs. We never need to make a phone call or leave a voicemail again, thanks to messenger apps. Hallelujah!

I bet it would be entirely possible to shun all human contact forevermore! Our social fitness could fade away to zero until we were 100 per cent bona-fide hermits! Lonely, yes. Comfortable and convenient, definitely.

Tribe vibes

No matter what you're into – no matter how niche or specific – there's a tribe of people just like you, somewhere out there. And the brilliant thing is, with the internet there to connect you, there's no need to engage in small talk or even show your face. Bliss.

As someone who has moved to new cities and countries, finding people online with a similar hobby to me has led to new friendships and social groups. It has helped me break down the social awkwardness of a first meeting.

Chloe

Hiding behind your computer screen, an alias and maybe even an avatar, you're free to be whoever you want. Nobody can see if you're blushing or shaking or feeling nervous or awkward.

I attended a social event called 'Frocktails' – a cocktail event for people who love to sew their own clothes. I didn't know anyone before the event but because I had made a few Instagram connections beforehand it helped me feel confident enough to attend. Getting to know some of the attendees on Instagram also meant that I was armed with a few things to talk about.

Renee

And the beauty is, you can tip tap tip tap type your way to connections safely and comfortably. Each word can be carefully considered. There's no pressure to speak in the moment – you can take your time. You can warm up and prepare what you want to say. Finding your voice is a lot easier online. You can delete, draft and rewrite. It's socialising, shy style.

I do find anonymous online talking a lot easier than in person, because they can't see me stressing out and I have a bit more time to think of a good reply.

Lauren

And we're not limited to the couple of hundred people who go to our local pub or live on our street. We're not lumbered with the people in school or at work. Whether you're a coffee connoisseur, a cross-stitch aficionado, a baton-twirling buff or a chicken-nugget nut, your tribe is out there waiting to 'meet' you. You can chat to them in forums or online groups, ensconced safely at home, behind your computer screen.

Social media is positive for shy people because you can interact and observe while in a 'safe place' and you can leave when you want. It's non-committal.

Brooke

No more awkward moments as you ask a random stranger if they're into New Wave French Cinema and just hope for the best. The fact that they are a paid-up member of the French Film Club means you can be pretty damn sure they know their Godard from their Truffaut.

Heaven.

Sure, others might find our very niche forums a bit odd or weird, but whatever. People may judge us for making friends online. But if it makes you happy to talk about manga cartoons, drum and bass, or UFC all day with people, then do it. You might use the internet as a way to build up to meeting people face to face, or perhaps your relationships will stay firmly online.

The world is changing. It's not weird or nerdy to network online. It's no longer the reserve of geeks who like Dungeons & Dragons. Consider the number of people who are making millions online. Consider online influencers. Fitness gurus. All with their tribes. Bringing people from all over the world together. In fact, we shy people were onto something. We saw and welcomed the potential of WiFi with open arms, knowing it would give us power, enabling us to communicate and socialise in our own quiet way. We were ahead of the curve.

I remember when I was thirteen and using MSN messenger, I discovered it was easy to type things that I found difficult to say. But I also made a real effort to say those things in real life. I thought, if I can type it, then I can say it.

Rebecca

On the one hand, hanging out online suits us shy people perfectly. But I do wonder if the fact that we can sidestep face-to-face conversations means we're not keeping socially fit, we're not practising socialising and we can easily lean out and away from human contact, contributing to a rise in shyness. Food for thought. (But let's not go out. Shall we order in?)

Unmuted in meetings

I'm not a fan of meetings. For so many reasons. All that sitting around a table with a bunch of scary people, while I'm overthinking everything, waiting for ages for my turn to talk and fearing being put on the spot.

Maybe that's why I love online meetings. Yeah, being on camera is way worse than sending a message or making a phone call. But compared with having to speak up face to face with a crowd of actual people, I'll take a Zoom any day.

For a while, I became obsessed with my own face. I was fixated on my wrinkles and blemishes and distracted by the gurning expressions I make when I talk and think. And then I discovered I can simply press a button and remove my self-view. Boom.

Nowadays, I have this whole virtual meeting thing down pat. I love how much I can control. I press a button and it touches up my appearance, so even on a rough day, I look good. I wear joggers and slippers or pyjamas, and as long as I don't have to stand up, nobody has a clue. I have notes and prompts on my desk, so nobody knows I have prepared to within an inch of my life. Plus, if I want to hide, I can simply turn off my camera.

And you can't really tell I'm nervous on Zoom. My body language is mainly invisible. I can sit back in my chair and shrink away into the background. And the chat function means we can even make our point in writing, without needing to speak at all. Result.

But is all this really a good thing? If we hide, all our ideas and thoughts and insights stay hidden too.

Without effort, we could simply slide into the shadows, masked up and anonymous, our cameras turned off. We can communicate from behind a screen, hardly needing to speak if we don't want to. We could lean back in our swivel chairs and avoid all social contact, relying instead on the online world and the robots in our lives.

Technology, such as social media, apps and tools are designed to be addictive, so we spend more time using them, sharing our data and viewing ads. They may as well be injecting dopamine into our forearms. But when the lure of our screens is far more appealing than our favourite person sitting next to us on the sofa, there may be a problem.

Maybe it's not all bad, though?

We like being able to interact with robots sometimes. We like being anonymous if we want to be. We like the fact that we can interact with people in a way that doesn't make us sweat buckets. And if we get our kicks from forums and gaming and social networks, is that so bad?

Just as technology makes it easier for us to hide, it also helps us to connect and communicate in ways that work better for us. Surely that's a good thing? Given that we can often feel like we're living in a world not made for us and that we don't quite fit in, isn't it refreshing that some aspects of modern life actually work in our favour, making us feel more comfortable and connected?

SHY POINTS

- The internet and technological advances make it easy for us to avoid human interaction.
- Technology such as texting, social robots and video meetings do help us to connect more comfortably with others.
- Finding our tribe and making connections online works for shy people.

CHAPTER 6

SHY HAPPENS

I think the most important thing I've learned from my mom has been: you're human if you have fear, but you can't ever let it determine how hard you go at a situation. If anything, it should make you go harder – go for it all the way.

Camila Cabello, singer*

We were squished onto the precarious accident-waiting-to-happen makeshift stage, the rehearsal for our Christmas play in full swing. The teacher, Mrs Allen (one of my favourite teachers of all time), was attempting to turn our noisy rabble of a choir into something resembling a wall of sound.

'We've got a growler,' she said.

I'm pretty sure she wasn't referring to a large beer jug or a part of the female anatomy. I'm no musician, but I reckon the implication was that someone was out of tune, singing in a key that was significantly lower than would be considered ideal.

---

* https://www.bramptonguardian.com/whatson-story/7228432-camila-cabello-was-very-shy/

Naturally, I assumed it was me.

Looking back on it, this was possibly the most ridiculous assumption I have ever made. My voice is childlike. Soft, tiny; yes. But, gravelly, deep, rasping, growly – said nobody about my little voice, ever. Logic and reason in that moment, however, were entirely absent. I knew she was directing her comment at ME.

I'm not a good singer, but prior to this, I had assumed my voice was soft enough that nobody noticed. But after 'Growlergate', I figured my voice was so totally offensive to the human ear that it could not be heard again.

And so began the miming years. Even now, thirty years later, I mime along to 'Happy Birthday' at parties. It's completely ridiculous.

It seems like the memories of school performances, particularly Christmas ones, are the source of lots of trauma. I wonder if teachers have a clue. Teachers, if you're reading this: I know you're busy and stressed, but it's clear that school performances can have far-reaching life-altering consequences, and not the good kind!

This was just one of many shy points in my life. Things that happened, which I didn't question or think about. They just were.

I don't think I realised I was shy as a child. I was just little ol' me, living my life. I didn't really think about the way I behaved or the things I thought. I was too busy riding horses, reading about horses, dreaming about horses and making magazines about horses (and miming).

I didn't know I was a shy person. I had no clue. I knew there were things I didn't want to do, and things I preferred, but I didn't understand why. I lived my life, doing things, without really considering that they were a certain way, or that they could be any different.

It wasn't until I was a young adult attempting to make my way in the world, and sometimes struggling to achieve the things I'd set my mind on, that I started to think more deeply about my life.

What was this thing holding me back? Why did the mere thought of doing karaoke make me want to puke? Why did I hate socialising in big, noisy groups? Why am I terrible at tooting my own trumpet? Why am I so self-conscious all the time? And why does being the centre of attention bring me out in a cold sweat?

Once I became aware of my shy feelings, I started on this journey to understand my shyness. Over time, I learned to work with it, and own it. If only I had started sooner, I wouldn't have spent so many years feeling stuck. But hey ho.

Understanding where your shyness comes from is an important step in the process of becoming shy and mighty. Knowledge is power – shy power!

Even if you're shy and you feel isolated, you're not an island; you exist in a mish-mash of different worlds; your family, your school, your friends, your neighbourhood, your culture. And each and every day, as you weave your way through life, these different worlds have an impact on you.

There's no need to go digging around in your past if you don't want to, like some kind of anxiety archaeologist. This is not intended to be traumatic. However, in order to understand shyness, it can be interesting to look at some of the things that you experienced as a kid, so that when you see them now, in this moment, you can assess whether you need to carry them with you for the rest of your life. Perhaps when you reflect on the roots of your shyness, you will recognise patterns, or realise that you can move past what happened, forgive and leave certain things firmly in the past.

Does the bond we have with our parents impact shyness?

When we're babies, we need our parents to survive. Unable to get a job, cook pasta for ourselves, or drive to the shops, we're heavily reliant on grown-ups. Bite the hand that feeds us? I don't think so.

My good friend, and all-round magnificent woman, Professor Karen Pine, explained this to me, so I could share it with you:

A possibility to consider is that the child's attachment style, and the initial form of attachment bond with a parent, may be related to shyness in later life, because a child needs, more than anything, to have a secure attachment bond. And that attachment involves having a parent or primary caregiver who is emotionally available to them, who makes the child feel seen and heard. If the child feels seen and heard and forms a strong attachment, then they are likely to grow up believing that others will be willing to see them and hear what they have to say.

However, in some cases it's possible that this emotional attunement doesn't occur and the attachment bond is not secure. The child may learn that the way that they are is not acceptable to the parent.

If they make a noise, or whinge or cry, or they allow their authentic self to come through, this possibly threatens the attachment and makes the adult more distant, less attuned, and less emotionally available.

A child or an infant can't think or understand why this is. They don't know that their parent has had a bad day, or has their own problems going on. The child might get the message that, in order to keep securely attached to the primary caregiver, to maintain the attachment bond, they might have to suppress their authentic self. They might learn that being quiet and undemanding and undemonstrative keeps the parent close to them. It's a toss-up between authenticity or attachment. And because humans are born helpless and dependent on a caregiver, they will always choose attachment over authenticity.

We choose to keep quiet, in order to survive.

How does family life impact shyness?

Aside from any genetic predisposition to shyness, spending our formative years in close quarters with shy or anxious parents who behave in an inhibited, fearful way towards their kids and the world outside is bound to have an impact on our own feelings and behaviour. Their anxiety rubs off on us.

Both my parents were shy, and from a very young age, I had the feeling that they wouldn't be able to stand up for me because they were shy, not strong.

Silke

Babies and infants need to be loved, seen and heard and cared for. Parenting is not just about strength and discipline. There is absolutely no reason why a shy person is not equipped to be a fantastic parent.

Dodging confrontation and difficult conversations are not exclusive to us shy folk. Many people fear and lack the skills to handle conflict. If, from a young age, we see our parents negotiating and discussing challenging topics in a calm manner, without violence, fear or aggression, we experience how to go about it. Without this kind of role modelling, we miss out.

If you don't get this kind of positive exposure, it's not game over! It's just a set of skills, not a blueprint set in stone. We have a lifetime of learning and development ahead of us. If you missed out, maybe it's time to start.

The family unit is like a little ecosystem, with its own rules, routines and rituals, as well as its own power dynamics and limitations. Being part of a family means rubbing along in close proximity with a bunch of other people, whose personality traits and behaviours are bound to shape ours.

It's hardly surprising, therefore, that family can impact how we feel about ourselves, our beliefs and behaviours, even many years after we've left home.

> *I believe I am a product of my family; being the youngest with a very extroverted boisterous sister and mother, it was hard to ever grow a voice of my own and be comfortable with myself.*
>
> Kelly

We've seen that shyness and social anxiety can be inherited from our parents. Clearly, this is not the case for everyone, and you might read this and think, erm, no way – my family aren't shy at all. But it seems that for many people, shyness does run in the family.

If your parents are worried about you mixing with others, attending parties, travelling on the school bus, going on the school trip or being in the football team, you're going to feel a sense of anxiety too. Being shrouded in a cloud of anxiety will make anyone sensitive to danger, fearful of social situations and wary of new people. And when you feel like that, you're less likely to want to get stuck in, stay out late, speak up or join in.

> *My dad was a great worrier and my mum was quite shy. I think my parents were anxious, like my whole extended family were, because although white-skinned, they had strong accents and were sometimes in awkward situations that made them feel different.*
>
> Kai

Kids who grow up in a secure, snug and happy home, filled with love and warmth and praise and comfort, are less likely to experience stress and anxiety and loneliness. When children feel unsure or insecure around their parents it can create social difficulties and anxieties as they grow up.

Controlling, highly critical or dominant parenting can also lead to shyness in kids. The rule of an iron fist is bound to make us shrink, stay silent and hide away for fear of reprisals.

> *My parents never encouraged my brother and me to speak or have opinions. Any accidents were ridiculed too. I feel I'm introverted and much prefer my own company now, or that of animals.*
>
> Isaac

Shyness is rooted in fear of judgement. So, living with authoritarian, manipulative or overly intrusive parents, who dominate, criticise and take away our power, fans the flames.

As a former military man, my dad was very domineering. He thought kids should 'hop to'. I think this contributed to me doing what I'm told and keeping my mouth shut.

Ashling

Growing up, scared to speak up or stand up for ourselves, makes us want to retreat into our bedrooms, and into our heads. This impacts the way we behave as adults too.

The trouble is, the more kids hide away, the more detached and harder to connect with they become. The distance grows and grows.

Having a father who could be bolshy and who saw shyness as a failing has probably made it worse for me, although I am sure that was never his intention.

Rosario

Does a stressful childhood make us more shy?

My dad died when I was a child. As ridiculous as it sounds, on top of the obvious grief, it was really embarrassing. It makes you different from your peers at a time when you don't want to stand out. Plus, I think it made me very cautious and sensible, which held me back.

Arthur

Shyness in kids has been shown to be linked to the levels of stress in the home. Growing up in a challenging family situation where parents are arguing or struggling to make ends meet can have an impact on shyness. Experiencing the world as a small kid can be confusing and scary, and handling traumatic experiences such as illness, divorce, moving or bereavement when you're young can be catastrophic. These events on their own would be enough to cause distress and grief, but combined with a predisposition towards shyness, they can cause a big kaboom.

We came from India to London and arrived on a foggy, cold winter night and I was scared. Everyone looked pasty and green to me. Everything looked eerily different. I think that's where my anxiety came from.

Indira

Where stress exists, kids are more likely to keep their feelings and worries to themselves because they don't want to add to their parents' problems. In those situations, kids feel isolated from their peers, with fewer opportunities to socialise, perhaps because of money or family rules. This can lead to being excluded or rejected by other kids, or to feeling unable to connect with others, causing increased feelings of loneliness, self-consciousness and low self-worth. And, these feelings of isolation feed back into the vicious shy-cycle of shyness. Isolation leads to anxiety, which leads to negative self-talk, which makes us hide, which makes us feel isolated, which loops us back round to feeling anxious again.

Could a difficult school experience lead to shyness?

I remember going to secondary school for the first time, walking up the stairs to my new class, thinking, this is it – this is my chance to do things differently, be more positive, less shy. I walked into the room, saw all the people, immediately went bright red and hid by the wall. I was so ashamed and annoyed that I just couldn't beat it.

Sarah

The petri dish of school life, with all its hustle and bustle, competition, cliques and teams, the pressure to speak up and perform, plus the self-consciousness of puberty, makes it the perfect breeding ground for shyness. Even without anything particularly bad or traumatic happening, the school experience can make us want to hide away and shrink under the desk until we graduate.

Perhaps you remember a particular school-based incident, like 'Growlergate' (see pp. 73–74) – even something seemingly minor, which shaped your self-worth and set you on the path of shyness. Perhaps someone made a comment that shamed or embarrassed you. Perhaps you were forced to speak up in class and your words got stuck in your throat. Perhaps that moment was enough to make you vow never to speak in class again, for fear of further humiliation.

Or perhaps, like my mate Harriet, you had to give a presentation in French. In France. In front of French people, about a really complicated aspect of linguistics. Perhaps the stress of it was too much and so you started sweating, your voice disappeared to nothing and you just kind of stood there, panicking. And, after that, you decided that public speaking wasn't for you.

Or maybe, like me, you had a traumatic language-lab experience that made you want to spend the next thirty years of your life hiding away.

Bullying has been linked to shyness and social anxiety. But here's the kicker, people who are more socially anxious and seem quieter are more likely to be targeted in the first place.

Scientists plonked a mouse bully in with a bunch of mice that were living their best life for a few days. I feel bad for the mice, to be honest, but let's assume the scientists didn't let anything really bad happen, and they were given lots of cuddles afterwards.

Anyway, the brains of the mice that were bullied by the mean mouse were checked out (hopefully, while they were still alive) and found to have increased levels of a hormone called vasopressin. This stressed-out hormone ramped up the brain receptors sensitive to social stimulus, and the bullied mice made a decision to steer well clear of other mice in general. Well, you would, wouldn't you? If I was stood face to face with a mouse bully, with bulging muscles and a mean look on his face, I too would make a mental note to avoid hanging out with mice I didn't know, in case they tried to steal my pocket money.

The more you hide, out of a desire for self-preservation, the more they sniff you out and come for you. Like the mean mouse stalking its next victim, bullies hone in on people who are less assertive, less likely to fight back and more likely to crumble. They seek out those who are alone, and not surrounded by bodyguards. They target people who are too shy and scared to squeal and rat them out. It's a terrible triangle of torture.

Being bullied trashes our self-esteem; it leads to isolation, loneliness, withdrawal, anxiety, depression and, of course, extreme shyness.

Bullying at school made me self-conscious of just about every physical aspect of me. When I look back, I see a pretty little girl, but it took me many years to get over their harsh words. It breaks my heart that I felt like a greasy mark that needed to be rubbed out.

Mo

Scientists have shown that up to 35 per cent of people have been victims of bullying.* Let's just take a moment to wrap our heads around

---

* K.L. Modecki, J. Minchina Allen, G. Harbaugh, N.G. Guerra and K.C. Runions, 'Bullying Prevalence Across Contexts: A Meta-analysis Measuring Cyber and Traditional Bullying', *Journal of Adolescent Health*, vol. 55, no. 5, November 2014, pp. 602–611.

that. A third of us experience fear and trauma as kids. Childhood is meant to be safe and fun.

Bullying is not a rite of passage, or a normal part of the school experience. It's not something that's easy to get over and leave behind, along with scabby knees, bubble gum, pimples and swings.

Being bullied can have a crushing and enduring impact on our mental health, causing a wide spectrum of issues, including anxiety, PTSD, rage, low self-esteem, depression and social anxiety. Kids who are bullied are more likely to need therapy or even psychiatric treatment as they progress into adulthood. These mental health issues don't dissolve when we leave school, they can continue to have a ruinous impact for years and years.

As a child our personalities are still developing, which is why being bullied as a kid can smash up your self-esteem.

Being abandoned by your peers and left to face the abuse alone extinguishes trust in other humans, possibly forever. Victims may withdraw socially and hide away at home, making it harder for them to socialise and make friends, throughout their lives.

In particular, if nobody stands up for you and helps you out when you're being bullied, your mistrust of other humans is cemented. And that can last a lifetime.

Cuts and bruises heal. Time moves on, but the wounds and hurt caused by bullying can leave hidden scars that don't fade easily.

Puberty is the cherry on the cake

Adolescence is a greasy, messy, gangly, emotional, stinky time. All those changes. All that hair! It's no wonder we become self-conscious and awkward, worried about the way we look, and whether our bits are big or small enough. We worry about fitting in, about looking the part, about our changing bodies – about everything! And we have so many hormones pumping around us, it's a wonder we can get through the day.

> *Growing up, I didn't fit the stereotypical mould of what girls should look like, so this didn't help my insecurities. The media was full of women and girls looking a certain way, which I didn't fit into.*
>
> Annushka

Fumbled attempts at flirting can take our self-consciousness and awkwardness to new heights. We hide our shyness behind a mask of eyeliner and mascara or dull our nerves and worries with drugs and booze. We lollop around, leaning on walls, avoiding eye contact, hiding beneath layers and fringes and trying to blend into the background, keeping quiet for fear of total humiliation or rejection.

I think my preference for flomping around in big, baggy clothes started as a teenager and was triggered when some helpful person commented loudly about my curves. I'm sure it was meant as a compliment, but it made me want to die. And to this day, I still feel very self-conscious about my figure – like somehow, it's too much and my curves need smoothing out or squashing down.

SHY POINTS

- Understanding where shyness comes from can help us to move past our fears.
- A number of factors can intensify our feelings of shyness:
  - Family life
  - Anxious parents
  - Dominant parents
  - Stress at home
  - School life
  - Bullying
  - The challenges of adolescence

CHAPTER 7

SHY SPY

I hate when people ask me, 'Why are you so quiet?' Because I am. That's how I function. I don't ask others, 'Why are you so noisy? Why do you talk so much?'

Anonymous

I spent most of my teenage years covered in mud, trying to control big, hairy horses, who often had other things on their mind. No matter how keenly I wanted to negotiate a series of brightly painted fences with style and panache, things did not necessarily go according to plan. Horses might love jumping, but they also love eating grass, seeing their friends and snoozing. Horses are huge. And I was not. Unless we both wanted to do the same thing, it wasn't gonna happen and I'd end up getting flung through the air on my own. Ouch.

In their book *Switch*, Chip and Dan Heath compare the conscious and the subconscious mind to an elephant and its rider. Now, I haven't ridden many elephants, but it seems to me we can compare the subconscious mind to a very obstinate horse, and our conscious mind to the rider. Unless they are both aligned, you're not getting anywhere fast. You might think you want to stand up on stage and give a talk in front of 500 people, but unless you want to do it consciously *and* subconsciously, it's going to be hard to make it happen. Both parts of your mind need to want the same thing – both must be pulling in the same direction.

You know in your conscious mind that singing on stage is not going to kill you. There are no sharks, lions or samurai swords involved. Rationally and logically, you know this. Using your conscious mind, you can put things in place to help you make it happen, like taking singing lessons, choosing a song to sing and finding a stage.

But making your goal happen is going to prove problematic if your subconscious mind is not playing ball. Your subconscious is the emotional side of you, and like a hefty horse, it's very stubborn and powerful. You can't make a horse do something it doesn't want to do. It doesn't matter how much the rider flaps about, if the horse is not feeling it, you're gonna end up in a heap on the floor.

Our brains are keeping us safe

I had landed the job of my dreams, working in marketing for a health and beauty company, and could not have been more excited (and not just because of the subsidised canteen and amazing freebies). Apparently, they needed someone with fresh ideas; someone with a bit of a rebellious streak who was going to shake things up, strategise outside the box, do some blue-sky thinking, run things up the flagpole, yada yada . . .

But from the moment I set foot in the office, it became apparent that my big plans for a shake-up were going to be stifled. I had been positioned – and this can't have been an accident – opposite a more experienced woman who had been with the company for over thirty years. Longer than I had been on the planet. She lived and breathed the business. It was her life, her passion, her raison d'être. She was completely obsessed with her job, but she was also counting down the days until she could retire and live by the sea. I guess it was ultimately a destructive, toxic, all-consuming love affair between her and the business.

It seemed to me that this woman – we'll call her Amy – whom I was sat opposite, was there to keep me in check and stop me from taking any unnecessary risks. How do I know? Well, every time I had an idea, she would crush it with this classic line:

'We tried that in 1983. And it didn't work.'

If she had a mic, she would have dropped it. Instead, she would adjust her glasses on their chain, and get back to her spreadsheets. Oh, those endless spreadsheets nearly killed me.

Looking back, I can see the funny side. As annoying as she was, and as much as I wanted her to hurry the hell up and retire, I can only imagine how annoying she found me, poor woman.

Amy didn't like risk, or the unknown, or anything unusual or uncertain. She wanted the team, the brand, the business, to tick along in a calm and uneventful manner, so that she could swing into retirement as quickly and painlessly as possible.

Sitting opposite this woman, day in day out, was like coming face to face with my own shyness: a controlling, and often negative force, trying to hold me back. All those restrictions and limitations did help our team avoid risk and stay secure and comfortable. But goodness, it was suffocating.

And sitting opposite a negative force dragged me down. It sucked the energy and sparkle from my bones. I felt thwarted. I didn't want to be protected or kept so small. I had so many concepts and opinions buzzing around my brain. Sure, I wasn't keen on the idea of presenting my work in meetings, raising my profile in the organisation or travelling to far-flung places on my own, but I was eager to do creative work and have new ideas and push the business forwards.

After a year or so, I left that organisation. I just couldn't hack being suffocated like that.

Lifting the lid on the shy brain

In order to work with our shyness, rather than letting it control us, we need to look under the surface, beyond how shyness feels and how we behave when we feel shy. Perhaps if we can get to grips with our grey matter, we can learn to work with and around the challenges it chucks in our path.

The amygdala is a little almond-shaped part of our brain, which functions a bit like a burglar alarm, sensing danger and alerting us when something dodgy is afoot.

Imagine a tiny Amy from the office, with her glasses on a chain and her hair in an excruciating-looking bun, living inside our brains. Amy is like a protective aunt, with a nose for danger and a penchant for risk assessment. Amy is not being a pain on purpose; she's trying to protect us. If we were to think about leaping off a building, jumping through a burning hoop on a motorbike or fighting an angry lion, Amy would put her foot down. Our brains are trying to keep us alive, and they do that by detecting potential threats, keeping danger at bay and encouraging us to behave in a more cautious way.

But here's the thing with our Amy, she tends to overreact. Amy notices every single piece of potential peril, and she doesn't keep it to herself. She calls her mate, the cerebral cortex, which is like the brain's control centre, in charge of deciding what we need to do next.

That's when our nervous system kicks into action, getting our body ready for what it thinks is imminent death from a perceived threat – say, a hungry lion! The nervous system sounds the alarm, turns on the sprinklers and activates the panic-room door, which is why we start sweating and shaking, and our hearts starts bashing through our chests.

This physical reaction triggers our conscious mind, which gets panicky and starts focusing on the physical symptoms. It may not feel like it, but our brain and our body are working together to try to keep us safe. It's the fight-or-flight response. Our bodies and our brains are in a heightened state of arousal, adrenaline pumping hard, so that we can either bash the lion, or leg it.

The chances are, however, that you're not facing off with lions on a regular basis. It's more likely that when you feel shy, you're worried about stuff that impacts your sense of self. Perhaps you're worried about talking to someone you like, or having a meeting with someone in authority, presenting your work, or having to stand up for your beliefs. Perhaps you're worried about making a mistake, about being judged, being dismissed, or feeling a sense of shame or embarrassment. You're not in grave danger. You're not going to be chopped into tiny pieces and eaten.

But none the less, your brain triggers a physical reaction to protect you from danger. Your palms get sweaty because your body is trying to cool you down. Your tummy goes jumbly, because your brain is advising against sitting down for a three-course meal, because you have a lion to fight, after all. It's also trying to quickly digest the food you've already eaten, so that you have more energy to fight that lion. You get a dry mouth and stumble over your words, because energy is being diverted away from your mouth to more useful areas. You feel light-headed because the blood is rushing to your arms and legs, where it's needed, so you can punch the lion and then do a runner.

You might avoid eye contact and hunch your shoulders. This submissive body language tells the lion that you're really very small and non-threatening, and hardly worth snacking on. It's an inbuilt way of telling your enemies that you're just little ol' you, and you're not a danger to them at all.

But here's the thing. A meeting is not the same as a lion. A slightly awkward conversation with someone at a bar is not a duel. A presentation is not a fight to the death. Your colleagues are (probably) not going to punch you in the face if you share your ideas in a meeting!

Thank you, Aunt Amy, for taking care of us. You're very sweet, but maybe you could focus on those spreadsheets, so we can get on with living our lives.

Constantly on high alert

It's sensible to be wary and a little cautious when faced with something new or unusual. But, what if we take it too far?

When I was a horse-mad teenager, my horse, Storm, was a sensitive soul. He was easily spooked and prone to catastrophising. A carrier bag fluttering in a hedge was an ogre ready to pounce. Dustbins waiting to be emptied were menacing monsters.

Because Storm had a propensity to do mad stuff, I was always on high alert. I became super aware of any oncoming threat or drama. I could spot a potential carrier-bag incident a mile away. I could read traffic and predict when someone might forget to indicate, or not give us enough space. I could smell danger.

The trouble was, I started to read danger when there was none. We'd be walking along, clip clop, clip clop, and I'd imagine we were going to meet an untimely death because there was a bird tweeting in the tree. And because I was building this stuff up in my mind, it started to take over. I was anxious all the time.

Shyness is like that. We can become oversensitive to danger. Even when there is none. When we are simply sharing our ideas in a meeting, the sense of danger is overwhelming. And the feeling of dread and fear and anxiety lasts and lasts. All that thinking about the possibility of danger, that may or may not happen in the future, affects how we feel in the present.

But it's not just future planning that causes our anxiety; it's also the past.

Memories and past experiences

Our brains are like a filing cabinet, crammed full of memories. We remember awkward, scary and uncomfortable things and file them away, just in case. We store information about when and where our fears and anxieties happened. Parties, meetings, classes, presentations . . .

There is a bunch of cells in our brain, near the amygdala, called the hippocampus, which is like our brain's librarian. It pulls out the files of our past experiences and traumas when something similar happens.

The hippocampus in our brain is in cahoots with Amy, our amygdala. They chat. The hippocampus nudges Amy the amygdala and says, we tried that in 1983 and it didn't work. See, look at this file. And that's when Amy the amygdala hits the panic button.

Partly because we're finely tuned to danger anyway, and looking out for it, and partly because we're drawing on past memories, we already feel fearful before anything scary or bad has happened. So, any time we come face to face with a situation that scared us in the past, perhaps where we might be put on the spot, or have to speak in front of others, meet new or intimidating people, or do something where people might judge us, we feel anxious and worried before we even begin.

The trouble is that the categories in our filing system are too broad. Just because one time you went to a party and felt self-conscious doesn't mean that you should feel anxious about all parties for ever more. Stamping 'Danger' on all kinds of memories in big red capitals stops us from moving forwards with our lives.

Our interpretation of events

The other day I was chatting to my brother, Ben, about our childhood and marvelling at the highs and lows of teenage mood swings. So grouchy and ragey. 'I'm sure I was never like that,' I said.

Oh how he laughed.

'Erm,' he said. 'Are you delusional?' OK. He didn't actually say that because my brother is way more polite than that. I think he probably, ever so slightly, raised an eyebrow.

It turns out that his memory of me as a kid is not the same as mine. Whaaat?! Apparently, I wasn't as cool, calm and collected as I recall.

We were both there, living the same reality. The same time and place, but different experience. Different memories. Different emotions. Different beliefs.

Everything is open to interpretation. We shape our feelings, our reactions, our behaviours and our memories based on the meaning we attach to events.

And the reason this is relevant here is that for many people, shyness can be triggered by an event or experience. Or rather, their interpretation of an event, and the meaning that they attach to it can influence their feelings and behaviour.

As far back as I can remember, I've had a really strong sense of resistance in certain situations, mainly to do with being seen and being successful. I couldn't really explain it or put my finger on it, but I've always had this sense that I couldn't do things, or that something was stopping me. It wasn't logical. Even in situations where rationally I *knew* I was capable, I would still feel resistant to putting myself out there.

I decided to try hypnosis to see if I could pull up some interesting files from the darkest depths of my filing cabinet and discover where my feelings of resistance come from.

Under hypnosis, my subconscious mind presented me with some scenes. They just kind of popped up, like files that were handed to me by the librarian at random. These thoughts were buried so deep down in the caverns of my grey matter, that, had I been fully conscious, I would never have been able to find them.

In one scene, I was about four years old and had just started primary school. Ben and I were in the same class, but I was standing alone, looking for a book in a huge expanse of bookshelf. I was worried and wasn't sure what to do. I didn't know who to ask or how to find what I needed. I felt alone, lost and on the edge. I looked for Ben, and at first, I couldn't find him, but then I spotted him on the other side of the classroom with the teacher and a bunch of other kids. I felt like nobody could see me, that I wasn't important and that I didn't matter any more.

Now, on the face of it, nothing bad happened. I was looking for a book and I couldn't find it. So what? I was fine.

But I attached meaning to the negative feelings in those tiny moments, telling myself I would always be isolated and on the edge, that other people are special, that they have things I want but can't have and that other people matter more than me.

The way we interpret events and experiences, even tiny things with no apparent significance, can impact us in a major way, leading us to create limiting beliefs, which we then choose to carry around with us forevermore.

During the process of hypnotherapy, we worked on transforming these feelings and beliefs, so that I can move forwards. We turned my cloak of invisibility into a cape of invincibility.

Shyness is a sensible reaction

Shyness comes from our innate desire for self-preservation.

When we feel shy, our brains are trying to keep us safe. It's normal to feel cautious in new and uncertain situations. It's smart to draw on past experiences and make calculated judgements and decisions. And it's prudent to listen and observe before we leap into action. Only an idiot would jump into a situation without checking if it's safe to do so first. Those are the people who will definitely get eaten by lions!

But most of the situations we find ourselves in are not life-threatening. Giving a talk is hardly hazardous and speaking up in a meeting probably won't involve grave danger.

It's when we attach negative meaning to our experiences and allow our subconscious to take over that we give our brain the power to stop us living our life.

SHY POINTS

- Shyness comes from our brains trying to keep us safe.
- In order to move forwards, the conscious and subconscious parts of our brains need to be aligned.
- Shy people are too sensitive to danger. There are no lions in meetings.
- We file away our memories to help us manage risk.
- The meaning we attach to our experiences can create limiting beliefs.
- Allowing our fears to take over stops us from living our lives.

CHAPTER 8

SHY, NOT SICK

If you're anything other than an [extrovert], you're made to think there's something wrong with you . . . That's like the story of my life . . . Coming to realise that about myself was very empowering because I had felt like, Oh my god, there must be something wrong with me, because I don't want to go out and do what all my friends want to do.

Emma Watson, actor*

Do you know what really bugs me about being shy? It's the way that some people treat me like I'm ill, or I have some kind of horrible disease. Luckily, I'm in tip-top health (touch wood), so when people talk to me like that, there is a real temptation to punch them straight in the face.

For example, yesterday, I was being interviewed about my podcast. So far, so normal. Until the end, after the set questions, there was a super-awkward pause, followed by a lumpy change of tone. The interviewer kinda cocked his head to one side and asked me whether I was in a relationship. At first, I thought he might be coming on to

* https://www.thecontentwolf.com/life/the-struggles-of-an-introvert-in-disguise/

me, which was a bit weird, considering I was about twenty years older than him, but you know – I am fantastically fresh-faced and spritely, so really it could be an easy mistake to make. Anyway, I digress. He asked me if I was in a relationship, because, he clarified, I'm shy and he was wondering how that would work.

The interview had been going quite well until that point, but it certainly plunged into the depths of awkwardness after that. Seeing the pity in his eyes was not nice. I explained to him, softly, that I'm shy in certain situations, but not with people I trust, or am married to!

Being an introvert is not viewed as an illness. And yet, shyness is described as a 'social disease', even by famous authors, psychologists and shyness experts. Even his royal shyness, Philip Zimbardo (remember that 1970s shyness study? see p. 55), published a hugely influential article in *Psychology Today* in 1975 called 'The Social Disease Called Shyness'. And I thought he was meant to be on our side.

As a child, I used to buy a magazine once a week and I refused to speak to the shopkeeper when he spoke to me. He noticed and started mocking me for it. I hated it; it made me feel awful, and I stopped going into the shop. I didn't understand how my shyness could be the source of amusement for anyone. Throughout my life, I have been mocked and criticised for it. I have been made to feel like there is something wrong with me.

Eve

We know the statistics by now. Around half of all humans are shy, and pretty much every single person on the planet has felt shy at some point in their lives. We can't all be broken, can we?

Diagnostic creep

When a handful of influential experts get together on panels to review the parameters of diseases and illnesses, if they consider one to be too rigid or small, they can expand it to include additional symptoms, pre-symptoms or mild symptoms. By altering the definition, they can effectively be labelling healthy people as sick, and altering the lives of millions of people. This is called 'diagnostic creep'.

For example, in 2008, when the description of osteoporosis was changed, the number of older women suffering from this bone-crumbling disease suddenly increased from 21 per cent to 72 per cent.

Why would they do that? Why on earth would they label healthy people as sick? Oooh, I don't know, could it be, erm, money?

Yes. Money.

In 2003, a panel created the concept of 'pre-hypertension' or pre-high blood pressure. You can imagine how many more people now could then be prescribed drugs, who were previously just living their lives. Shedloads. And to make matters worse, 80 per cent of the panel members had financial links to companies marketing and selling drugs for high blood pressure. They were being paid huge sums of cash by these pharmaceutical companies for speaking gigs, doing research or consulting. Talk about a conflict of interest. What a scam!*

Diagnostic creep has been creeping all over shyness too.

In his eye-opening book, *Shyness: How Normal Behavior Became a*

---

* Raymond N. Moynihan, Georga P.E. Cooke, Jenny A. Doust, Lisa Bero, Suzanne Hill, Paul P. Glasziou, 'Expanding Disease Definitions in Guidelines and Expert Panel Ties to Industry: A Cross-sectional Study of Common Conditions in the United States', *PLoS Medicine*, vol. 10, no. 8 (2013), e1001500, https://journals.plos.org/plosmedicine/article?id=10.1371/journal.pmed.1001500

Sickness, Christopher Lane exposes the way the pharmaceutical industry has seized hold of shyness and turned it from a personality type or perfectly normal set of behaviours into a medical problem:

> Shyness isn't just shyness anymore. It's a disease. It has a variety of overwrought names, including 'social anxiety' and 'avoidant personality disorder', afflictions said to trouble millions (almost one person in five, according to some estimates).*

How did the pharma companies rebrand shyness as social anxiety?

In 1994, a bunch of American psychiatrists got together on a committee and added a load of new diseases to the uber-influential book *The Diagnostic and Statistical Manual of Mental Disorders* (*DSM*). This book, with its extra pages filled with all kinds of new illnesses, included our friend social anxiety.

For the new edition, they expanded the symptoms of social anxiety to cover the experience of bog-standard shyness – previously thought of as no more than a quiet, more reserved kind of person who doesn't love the limelight and gets stressed out by being the centre of attention.

According to the fifth edition of the *DSM*, social anxiety is:

> A marked fear or anxiety about one or more social situations in which the individual is exposed to possible scrutiny by others. Examples include social interactions (e.g. having a conversation,

---

* Christopher Lane, *Shyness: How Normal Behaviour Became a Sickness*, Yale University Press, 2007.

meeting unfamiliar people), being observed (e.g. eating or drinking), and performing in front of others (e.g. giving a speech).

The full definition encompasses many aspects of normal shyness, like fear of public speaking, concerns about being judged or messing up or saying the wrong thing. This definition makes it easy for half the population – anyone who is even a bit shy – to be diagnosed with social anxiety disorder, labelled as mentally ill and be prescribed drugs.

Lane points out that, although the *DSM* does warn professionals not to mix up shyness and social anxiety, it means nothing because the examples and definitions in the manual are so muddied and overlapping that it's impossible to separate the two.

This book is the bible of healthcare professionals, used by doctors and psychiatrists, as well as insurers, prisons and even universities. And, according to this dictionary, someone like me, who is awkward around people they don't know, or who gets nervous before public speaking, has social anxiety, which is a mental illness. As such, if I lived in the USA, I could therefore be prescribed pills like Zoloft, Paxil and Prozac.

The fact that a drug like Paxil can now be prescribed for shyness didn't just magically happen. Pharmaceutical company GlaxoSmithKline (GSK) knew that in order to sell more pills they would need to raise awareness of social anxiety by funding advertising campaigns, recruiting celebrity doctors and incentivising groups of patients to provide testimonials and stories for the media.

The Paxil launch campaign, ran with the slogan: 'Imagine being allergic to people'. Posters popped up all over America, saying, 'You blush, sweat, shake – even find it hard to breathe. . . That's what social anxiety disorder feels like.'

There was no mention of GSK though, or Paxil. Instead, the

campaign was positioned as a general awareness-raising campaign for social anxiety, featuring the badge of the (sham) social anxiety disorder coalition and its three non-profit members: the American Psychiatric Association, the Anxiety and Depression Association of America and Freedom From Fear. And because the campaign was not marketing medication, the posters were not required by law to mention Paxil's side effects – which include the shakes, nausea and lack of libido.

The advertising campaign also included a press release that claimed that social anxiety disorder 'affects up to 13.3% of the population' – one in eight Americans – and is 'the third most common psychiatric disorder in the United States, after depression and alcoholism'. A more realistic estimate would be around 2 per cent.

And it's no surprise that, as a result of this campaign, the size of the social anxiety market increased dramatically. And they sold heaps of drugs.*

Talk about dark. It's like a form of cognitive cleansing.

And with that kind of message permeating our institutions, it's no wonder the narrative around shyness is that it's a problem that needs fixing. Just pop these pills and you'll transform into a more acceptable human.

I would rather manage the negative aspects in non-medicinal ways. There are certainly times when I would take a confidence pill, if it existed, but I'm less keen on the side effects and trade-offs that come with medication.

Michael

---

* Brendan I. Koerner, 'First, you market the disease ... then you push the pills to treat it', *The Guardian*, 30 July 2002, https://www.theguardian.com/news/2002/jul/30/medicine-andhealth

Social anxiety has gone viral

The impact of this rebrand can be seen on social media, where magic cures, cyberchondria and drama are rife. Social media surrounds us with extremes, and shyness has been rebranded to fit in.

Looking at shyness through the lens of social media, you can see how it might seem a bit bland. But social phobia, or social anxiety? Now you're talking! Like, someone who has social anxiety is going to get taken a lot more seriously than someone who is just shy.

Back in the day, when I worked in marketing for a skincare brand, we held focus groups about sensitive skin. We recruited people who had sensitive skin to join these groups, so we could find out more about the challenges they faced. For example, flare-ups, itchiness, redness and so on.

But a strange thing happened. It became apparent that out of the ten people in each group, only one or two actually had sensitive skin. The rest were faking. Although they were wholly unaware that they were faking it, and were completely convinced they had sensitive skin.

As the discussions progressed, they would reveal details that contradicted their self-diagnosis. They'd talk about washing their face with basic bar soap or using really strong or fragranced products; things that nobody with sensitive skin would do because their face would fall off.

Were they there for the doughnuts, coffee and cash? Perhaps. Were they lonely and wanted a chat? Maybe. But why choose this particular focus group? I believe they liked the idea that they had something about them that was a bit delicate and vulnerable; something that needed special care and treatment.

Social anxiety is all over Instagram. As I'm writing this, the hashtag

#socialanxiety has been used around a million times, whereas the hashtag #shyness has been used just 80,000 times. That's quite a discrepancy. Especially, when you consider the fact that social anxiety is a serious challenge, and that it sits right at the far end of the shyness spectrum. It seems to me that there's a bit of a buzz about #socialanxiety, and it's turning us into a bunch of cyberchondriacs.

I wonder what's behind this. Perhaps the proliferation of hashtags has led to us labelling everything, and the accompanying algorithms encourage us to embrace current trends. Perhaps the fact that people are not feeling heard encourages us to turn to social media, and hashtags, to help us find and connect with people in a similar position. Maybe using clinical terms, which pathologise normal human behaviour, helps us to be taken seriously, and ultimately get the help we need.

When things are not going brilliantly, one way to get attention is to be doing terribly. If things are awful and you're struggling and your life sucks, then you get attention too; it may be a different kind of attention, but it's still attention. That could be why many shy people choose to see themselves as having social anxiety. Because being shy is mediocre. It's normal and boring. Rather than having good old boring shyness, they want the most dramatic version at the extreme end of the scale.

Shyness exists on a spectrum and there is no clear cut off-point when it turns into social anxiety. There's no big siren or flashing lights. Social anxiety. Alert, alert! Although, if there were, clearly it would be of no comfort whatsoever.

And, of course, many of the features of shyness mimic the symptoms of social anxiety, which makes it all the more confusing.

It's a good thing that we are all talking more about mental health and that anxiety has become destigmatised. But the fact that social anxiety has been reduced to memes and hashtags, and become normalised to such an extent makes it seem more fashionable, more palatable than shyness.

Lucy Foulkes, author of *Losing Our Minds: What Mental Illness Really Is – and What It Isn't*, describes chatting to students about their mental health and was surprised that anxiety and depression seemed to affect everyone! And yet, this seems unlikely.

What seems more likely – in universities, but also in schools, online and in private conversations – is that individuals in more hospitable parts of the mental health terrain have started to co-opt terminology that really needs to be reserved for people trapped further in its depths.*

On the downside

We shy bods do tend to assume the worst, and often believe things are worse than they really are. We can get stuck in a cycle of negativity, where we think everything is doomed.

When our shyness takes hold and we get into a negative pattern of thinking, we make assumptions that things are screwed for ever, that it's all our fault. We assume people are thinking bad things about us and that everyone is laughing at us. We feel like everything is difficult and rubbish, and we'll never get beyond our challenges. We set ourselves

---

* Lucy Foulkes, 'What We're Getting Wrong in the Conversation about Mental Health', *The Guardian*, 29 March 2021, https://www.theguardian.com/commentisfree/2021/mar/29/conversation-mental-health-psychiatric-language-seriously-ill

very high standards and can be really hard on ourselves if we mess up or fall short. We spend way too much time looking back and fixating on all our flaws and the way we messed up or looking forwards and worrying about all the scary bad things that might happen. We focus on the lows and ignore or explain away the highs.

For example, if we go to a party and find it hard to be all chatty and flirt our way around the room, we catastrophise and exaggerate and fixate on our failings. Instead of thinking about it logically and observing objectively, we decide that we are terrible at small talk, we're unattractive, nobody likes us, everyone thinks we're weird and we will never meet our soulmate because of our pathetic party performance.

In fact, we are the perfect target for a PR campaign to rebrand shyness as social anxiety. We are ripe for the picking. An extreme diagnosis taps into our tendency to catastrophise.

Shyness doesn't need medicating

Having a professional diagnosis for our experience helps us to carry our shyness into adulthood and be taken seriously and gives us a more palatable explanation for our feelings. Particularly when shyness is mis-understood and sneered at by so many. It can make it very tempting to want to move into a different camp.

Encouraging people who are struggling with mental illness to seek treatment is a good thing. I don't disagree with treating serious disorders like social anxiety with drugs. Of course not. Real social anxiety can be limiting and debilitating. It can have a massively negative impact on someone's life and can lead to depression, substance abuse and even suicide.

I was prescribed Adderall in college because I mentioned in passing to my doctor that I had a hard time paying attention in lectures. It did help me focus, but completely unexpectedly, it cured my social anxiety and totally changed my life. I still remember that feeling of freedom and try to mentally recreate it.

Colton

I am less keen on the idea of medicating something which is not an illness and cannot be fixed. Shyness is a normal human response. A normal personality type. Shyness is not a mental illness!

Shyness is not something to fix. We're all different and there's nothing wrong with it. There's not enough room for everyone to be gobby and outgoing.

Thandie

Feeling uncomfortable, awkward or anxious in certain situations – like when you're talking to someone in a position of power, when you're out on a date or you're giving a presentation on a big stage – is a normal human reaction. It's ok and normal to feel afraid or worried. Feeling like this doesn't mean you're broken and need to take drugs to dull your feelings.

There are other ways to work with shyness that don't involve taking medication. I believe that if we understand our shyness – why we feel and react the way we do – then we can figure out how to leverage it and turn it into a strength. Admittedly, some aspects of being shy make life more complicated, but others are a gift.

I would never take medication for my shyness. I believe that being shy is part of who we are. You can't cure YOU.

Logan

SHY POINTS

- Shy people are not sick, or ill or broken.
- By expanding the medical definition shyness has been repackaged as a disease that can be medicated.
- Drug companies have normalised and promoted social anxiety to sell more drugs.
- Social anxiety has become popularised – particularly on social media.
- An extreme diagnosis may make us feel seen and heard and comforted, but it might not be the right diagnosis.
- Shyness is a normal human reaction, not a mental illness.

CHAPTER 9

SHY'S THE LIMIT

Alone we can do so little; together we can do so much.
                    Helen Keller, author and activist*

Dorothy Hamill is an American figure-skating champion who captured the hearts of a nation in the 1970s with her elegant performances, her cool haircut and her quiet nature.

I was shy and really didn't want to talk to anybody. So, I fell in love with skating. It was where I could express myself and I ended up in my little cocoon.

                                        Dorothy Hamill†

Personally, I can't imagine anything more exposing than being a figure skater. Well, other than being a stripper. The idea of figure skating itself seems like a very chilly melting pot of challenges. Being graceful, for

---

* https://quoteinvestigator.com/2014/04/21/together/
† https://www.vailvalleymagazine.com/featured-stories/becoming-dorothy-hamill/

starters, is not my forte, and in the freezing cold, my red, runny nose and goosebumps wouldn't go with all those sequins.

Every move you make, every angle of your body is being critiqued and judged. And there are actual scorecards, with decimal points! The climate of competition seems to be off the charts. *I Tonya*, anyone? It's more ice queen than super chilled. The pressure and perfection wouldn't work for me – perfect skin, perfect hair, perfect make-up, perfect pointy toes. You don't see many messy, unruly ice skaters, do you? Plus, I can't skate, so that's an issue.

All that pressure to perform, constant evaluation and cut-throat criticism. And all those people watching – parents, trainers and your competitors – even during training sessions. Imagine the stress of the competitions, being judged like that. If you only get 6.23 for a triple toe loop, everyone will be slagging you off. Blimey, it's harsh. And to top it all off, if you fall over, you have to get back up again, gracefully, with a fake smile on your face, pretending that landing face-first on the ice didn't hurt at all.

I wonder what it would be like to be a shy figure skater; the judgement, competition and expectations mixed in with the complexities of shyness. Psychologists have actually investigated the plight of the shy figure skater. And it turns out, unsurprisingly, that it's pretty damn chilly out there on the ice.

Hmmm, I wonder why that might be? Well, let me tell you.

There are expectations; to have the right look, to live up to the hopes of your coach and family and friends. And knowing that people have made sacrifices and invested their time and money in you could make you feel ill at ease.

As shy people, we worry about being judged in everyday life, never mind when we are actually being judged. We're self-conscious, particularly when we're wearing a skin-tight outfit and being watched by highly critical competitors and audience members. In a cauldron of competition, we feel anxious and worry we're not good enough, or that we're going to make a mistake. We can get pretty down on ourselves.

> *I think I am quite competitive but, ironically, I always expect to come last – how messed up is that?*
>
> Lucy

Our competitive anxiety gives us physical symptoms, like puking and the shakes, which are not helpful when you're spinning around in the air, above a hard surface, wearing sharp blades on your feet. And it's a vicious circle, or triple axel, if you will. Because we're not confident, we are less likely to perform as well as we could. Shyness has been proven to affect an ice skater's ability to perform in competitions. And when you're zooming around on the ice in front of an arena of people feeling scared and nervous, there's plenty of scope to stack it and land on your arse.

Talking of falling, I know all about that. When I was competing in local horse-riding competitions, I would get so nervous that I would turn into a total brat. I'd snap at my poor mum, who had dragged herself out of bed at 5am on a weekend to help me. I'd feel sick beforehand, with a terrible tummy ache, and have some kind of asthmatic wheeze afterwards. I put so much stress on myself and my hairy horse, Storm, to do well – partly because I didn't want to let people down, and partly because I was so self-conscious about looking silly in front of everyone. And the one time my dad came to watch me, I ended up falling on my head, nearly breaking my neck, then wandering around semi-concussed, talking gibberish. He didn't come back to watch me again after that.

> *Growing up, I hated winning things because I didn't want the attention. Unless it was something that would make my teachers like me better, in that case, it was less about competition and more about pleasing authority.*
>
> Simon

Some people lap up the attention and limelight, but we shy people have mixed feelings about winning. We want to do well, but we also don't necessarily want the exposure and spotlight that accompany it. Winning means medals, but it also means ceremonies, interviews and cameras, with lots of people watching. And of course, winning means going to the next level and having to do it all again. Being mediocre is much more comfortable. And not entering the arena in the first place is the comfiest option of all.

The human race

Competition is everywhere. It's part of life.

From the moment we are born, we enter into the human race. We compare ourselves endlessly to see who's winning. Who can talk first, walk first, learn to ride a bike first, and so it goes on. We compete to get good grades, for attention from our parents, in sport, to win places in plays and on teams, to win races and matches. We judge each other and are judged all the way through adolescence, on social media and in real life. Everything is measured in likes and grades and numbers.

We compete to get into universities or colleges, to secure the best education and the best prospects.

And then, in the world of work, we compete to get the job, to win pitches and projects, to earn more money. Whether we're an accountant, a retail assistant, a lawyer, a coder, a hairdresser, a teacher or a builder, we battle against demands, deadlines and colleagues. We're measured, compared and appraised.

Socially, we compete to look the best, to win someone's heart, to have more sex, to be thinner, or taller, or bigger, or hotter or stronger. We compete to get the most views, the most shares, the most engagement, the biggest followings.

Incidentally, if you want to experience a highly charged competitive environment, head down to a kids' soccer match. There, you will witness all manner of judgement, criticism, rage, aggression, abusive language and violence. And that's usually just the parents.

The pressure to compete, to succeed and to win is everywhere. Survival of the fittest is firmly ingrained into our society. Even when we are relaxing, we compete for fun, in sport and games and pub quizzes.

I hate competitive situations; they make me feel really anxious. Even quizzes or board games with groups of people – I'd rather not take part as I think I'll lose. I hate competing with others in the workplace and think this was a factor in me going freelance; I don't have to compete with colleagues.

Caroline

It's one thing after another. We feel like winning will make us happy. We gaze at what other people have, and we want it; and then some.

The best body, the best home, the best job, house, car, holidays . . .
It's incessant. The human race is exhausting!

Competition gone completely crazy

My son Jacob likes to talk. Not always with me, or about the things
that I want to talk about, or at times when talking is actually appropriate. But still, he likes to talk.

As a baby, he was pretty chatty, which was both cute and alarming
at times, when he repeated things I'd just muttered under my breath
back to me.

One day, a friend boasted over a babyccino that her baby 'had 120
words'. She explained that every time the little squidge said a word,
they wrote it on the fridge.

I'll never forget that moment. She had 120 words.

What I had was absolutely no idea how many words Jacob 'had'.
I knew he liked to talk and could say some stuff. But the idea of
tracking his words and telling people about how many he 'had'
seemed like some next-level nonsense to me. I mean, we all learn
to talk eventually. What's the point of counting? And even if you
did decide to count, why the hell would you tell anyone else about
it?

But I couldn't quite let it wash over me in a serene fashion. I knew
it was ridiculous. And yet, I felt pressure to join the race.

Did I decide to track Jacob's words, give him booster lessons and see
if I could teach him Mandarin and Spanish, so that we could blow that
baby out of the water next time we went for a coffee? Nope. I didn't. I
told myself it was a slippery slope to some very strange behaviour, and
that we were far too busy walking endlessly around the park through

the driving rain in an attempt to get Jacob to sleep to bother with all that yummy mummy foolishness.

I didn't want to play. The pressure of a competitive situation felt oppressive and horrible. Plus, we would never win. And it would wind me up. So, I swerved the competition. I came up with some excuses and sidestepped it. I gave them a wide berth from then on.

Smart move, in this case, I think.

But what if discomfort around being ranked, measured and critiqued leads us to sidestep the stress and judgement of competition altogether? We fear failure and judgement. We assume we won't measure up and that we can't win. We don't fight for it. We walk away. And we hide.

One of my siblings is extremely successful (globally) and as much as I am very proud of him, I think growing up, the competitiveness affected me to a certain extent. Hence, I do retreat or find the arena less interesting.

Harry

When we step out of the arena, we can't possibly win. Our contempt for competition is not good for us, or for society.

In a land of opportunity, we miss out

I like not being noticed. It has been a struggle because I love performing, but if I'm in a group of people and someone has a bigger personality, I'm like, 'Go ahead, and have fun!' It looks like a lotta work.

Amy Adams, actor

Competition is hard-wired into some cultures. Living a shy life in a meritocracy, where everyone is out for themselves, can be particularly challenging.

America, for example, is the land of opportunity, where the culture of the individual dominates. Success is knowing what you want and going after it. Loud, charismatic big personalities reign supreme. Success, bravery and adventure are all part of the backbone of society. It's everyone for themselves, fighting to make it no matter what.

America was not built on fear. America was built on courage, on imagination and an unbeatable determination to do the job at hand.

President Harry S. Truman

This fierceness filters down and permeates every fibre of society, from school jocks and cheerleaders to the macho bro-culture in organisations. In cultures where loud, outgoing and alpha rules, shyness is seen as a problem. Where the culture revolves around individual success and competition, shy people are often perceived as failures: quiet oddballs.

We don't enter the arena, step out onto the stage, or onto the ice.

Be *your* best, not *the* best

So, what's a shy person to do? Well, one option would be to carry on hiding, and not participating. And that's fine if that's what you want to do. But what if you don't want to live your life in a shed, or under a blanket? What if you have skills and talents that you want to share with the world? What if you have a voice and something to say? What if you want to change the world?

There must be a way!

A sure-fire way to fail is to stop ourselves from even trying.

When I started writing this book, I spent a few months, erm, not writing this book. I became paralysed by the fear that my book would not be the best, and it cramped my creativity, big time. I was more blocked than a festival toilet.

Instead of writing, I spent my time trying to find the perfect place to write. I bought an array of new pens. And notebooks (enough to stock an entire stationery shop). I bought a new laptop. I bought some new shoes. I sat like a zombie on the sofa, scrolling through my social media.

I felt gripped by all kinds of feelings and insecurities. I felt like I was never going to measure up. Like I was a small, insignificant loser. I was doubting myself. Worried that people would think I wasn't good enough. That I was some kind of flake. I started making plans to jack it all in and lie in a darkened room for the rest of my life.

We shy people have high expectations of ourselves, and it gives us the perfect excuse to hide. If we're not going to be the best or win big, maybe we shouldn't even try. Sure, I could measure myself against book charts, and probably be disappointed in myself for not writing the bestselling book of all time.

Or I could approach things differently: just because this book may not be the only one on shyness, or the best one on shyness ever written, does that mean I shouldn't have bothered? On a bad day, I'm not sure. But this book is my take on shyness, and that's valid. This is the best book *I've* ever written about shyness.

And also, erm, this isn't actually a competition. It's a book. And hopefully, it's going to help a few people.

Likewise, life is not a competition. We are all just doing the best we can do. The point is, we all get to do stuff. We all get to participate and get involved.

If there is only one person who wins at life and everyone else who doesn't measure up just gives up and walks away, there wouldn't be anyone else left! If there was only one hairdresser in the world, the greatest hairdresser of all time, and everyone else shrugged, put down their scissors and decided to give up, how would we all get our hair cut? Does the fact that we are not being the best mean we should all give up? Nope.

When the pressure to be the best gets too much, it's not spurring us on, it's stopping us in our tracks before we've even got started. We can't be our best if we're doing nothing at all. Let's choose to focus on the things that matter to us instead. Doing *our* best. Enjoying what *we're* doing. And hopefully making a contribution as we do so.

Forget fame

Playing small is a positive thing if it means making a big difference.

Choose to be cherished by a small number of people and have a lasting impact on their lives, rather than a glancing impact on the lives of many; to be truly appreciated by a handful of people than have a million people click a like button mindlessly, in passing, because they quite like your shoes.

Take the shy little girl who took a stand against bullies, aged just three and a half. When the shy kindergartener spotted her little buddy was being bullied, she set down her fears and awkwardness and stood up for what was right. She wasn't in it for the fame, likes, recognition or rewards. In that moment, she simply knew she didn't like what she saw, and she wanted to change it. She wanted to right a wrong and stand up for what she believed in. Her shyness gave her empathy. It helped her to notice what was going on around her. And it made her mighty.

She took control of the situation, got the help she needed from the teacher. And in doing so, she created a big change for that little boy.*

The important stuff can't be measured. It's the goosebumps you get from knowing that someone has travelled across the country to hear you read a poem, the warmheartedness you feel because your project helped reunite an old couple or the pride you feel when you finally muster the courage to stand up on a stage, tell your story and change a young lad's life for ever.

I have to remind myself of this daily. It's so simple to get sucked into comparison and competition. All I need to do is hop online and the feelings of inferiority start creeping in. The fact that my stats are small, my audience is minute and my rankings are low gives my inner bully the perfect opportunity to start mouthing off.

Measuring ourselves against other people in a 'mine-is-bigger-than-yours' competition misses the point. When we know that what we're doing is making a difference to the people and things that are important to us, that's what counts.

Forget fame. Turn your attention towards impact.

Out of the in crowd

'Get into groups!' Argh. Those words send shivers down the spines of shy people. Working in teams and groups is not easy for us. We like silence and working independently. We like having peace and quiet to think and create. There's no battling to be heard or scrambling to speak up when you're working on your own. Speaking up and expressing our

---

* https://www.evansville.edu/changemaker/downloads/more-than-simply-doing-good-de-fining-changemaker.pdf

needs do not come easily to us. And in a group of people who don't stop talking, we often struggle to be heard.

The idea of being a lone ranger might seem more comfortable. But is it really preferable? When you're out there on your own in the big wide world, things can be daunting.

Whether you're a writer, a freelancer, an artist, a student, a business owner or an athlete, being a solitary shy person, struggling to make it when it's everyone for themselves, is not your happy place.

Trying to compete, succeed and win when you're all alone is exposing and scary. We shy away from comparison and judgement. And, there's a strong temptation to run a mile.

So, what's a shy person to do?

Community and collaboration over competition

In the 1970s, psychologist Philip Zimbardo and his colleagues went over to China to investigate shyness. In a dramatic plot twist, they couldn't find any shy kids in China. None. Given the fact that many Asian countries, like Japan or Taiwan, have high levels of shyness, this was particularly surprising. So, what made China different?

According to their reports, the communist ideology had, at that time, created kids who were quiet and docile, who worked hard and concentrated well. Rather than encouraging competition and battling against each other, everyone was encouraged to work together, in service to the state. The researchers observed that personal success and competition were less important than working together.

The Chinese schoolkids embraced the mantra 'Friendship first, competition second'.

It would appear that the Chinese cultural revolution has 'sacrificed' the values of student self-definition, individuality, originality and personal success for those of a collective identity, selflessness, service to the state, industry and uniformity. In so doing, they have also eliminated the cultural foundation which makes shyness possible and its development feasible.*

Clearly there are advantages and disadvantages to a communist regime. Cough. And based on my own research, nowadays, there are indeed a lot of shy people in China. But imagine how we quiet people might thrive in a society where friendship was the most important thing. We might not wish to embrace communism, but in our culture of competition, shy people can choose to run a different race. We can choose to embrace community and collaboration.

It takes me longer than the average person to feel like I belong. In workshop classes in college, for example, it could take almost half the semester to feel part of 'the group'. Once I felt a part, it was amazing!

James

What if winning was not the aim, and instead we worked together with people we like spending time with, towards a common goal? What if we pooled our knowledge and resources to create the most innovative and exciting ideas and solutions? What if we invited contributions from people with talents we admire, to create meaningful, long-lasting

---

* Philip Zimbardo, Paul Pilkonis, Robert Norwood, 'The Silent Prison of Shyness', Department of Psychology, Stanford University, 11 November 1977.

change? What if we gave each other a boost, instead of trying to win at all costs?

I joined a co-working space and organised regular Friday-night drinks; it was nice to feel a part of something and massively helped me reduce my panic attacks. I'd been stuck at home on my own for too long. I also joined a local networking group for small businesses and realised that I was in the same boat as a lot of other people, which really helped.

Lloyd

When a common purpose takes precedence over the ambitions of the individual, we feel comfortable and safe. We are more likely to thrive.

In a world where shy people feel isolated and alone, where our talents and attributes are not always appreciated, especially in meritocratic societies and competitive situations, it strikes me that we could come together and support each other instead of standing in opposite corners of the room all by ourselves.

I'm a virtual assistant, so I'm always working as part of someone else's team or supporting others. I like being part of a community and I work better that way.

Carly

Instead of worrying about whether we are as good as someone else, or if they're better than us, or wasting our energy wishing we were more like other people, we can focus instead on helping others – on being a member of a team, reaching out to other people and welcoming them in, giving others a voice.

If we embrace community and collaboration over competition, we could do things differently. We could build social enterprises and start community projects; or we could embrace different pricing models, where we buy one give one, or where a percentage of profits are donated to charity.

Let's measure ourselves based on the values that mean the most to us, rather than using someone else's measuring stick.

Friendship first, competition second

The competition in high-school baseball in the USA is killer. And the battle between Mounds View, a public high school in a Minneapolis suburb, and Totino-Grace, a neighbouring Catholic high school, was no different. Particularly when the prestigious Minnesota State Championship was on the line.

When Jack stepped up to bat for Totino in the dying moments of the game, he found himself stood across from star pitcher, Ty, who also happened to be his childhood friend. Talk about a no-win situation. Someone was going to go home a loser.

Ty fired the ball at his friend. Jack's bat whooshed past the ball and missed.

Strike! He was out. It was all over.

Ty and his team were victorious.

The crowd erupted. The entire team and coaching staff stormed the pitch, celebrating and leaping on each other in ecstasy.

But not Ty. Rather than joining his teammates in their festivities, he jogged over to his old friend Jack and gave him a huge bear hug, which lasted a full ten seconds. That's one long hug. (Personally, I think that's rather too long for a hug, but that's just me, ha ha.)

'I knew I had to say something,' he explained to Minnesota's Bring Me The News. 'Our friendship is more important than just the silly outcome of a game. I had to make sure he knew that before we celebrated.'

Despite the euphoria and the triumph, Ty knew what really mattered. The hug went viral and has since been seen by millions of people.*

Sometimes we need a reason that is bigger than ourselves and our fears to propel us forwards and give us the courage we need.

Take Jasmine, the girl I met hiding in the corridor when I was about to go on stage to give a school talk. She was there to receive a prize, but she couldn't face even going into the hall, which was bursting at the seams with students and teachers and parents. Even though she had won a prize for her work, she was struggling to make it into the room.

It seemed to me that nobody really understood. *Oh, she does that . . . she often stays outside the room.* I felt so sad that she was literally not in the room. That she was missing out.

I had a word with her. Because I understood. I remember hiding in the toilet myself, avoiding collecting a prize when I was at school. The idea of going onto the stage was just too much for me to handle.

She told me about her family who had come to see her. They would be so proud. The fact that her family would get so much pleasure from seeing her in the room and collecting her prize gave her the strength she needed to open the door and take a seat.

---

* https://www.npr.org/2018/06/12/619145417/after-a-high-school-baseball-game-a-hug-goes-viral?t=1618213608799

In my talk, I shared my own story, and the reason why I was doing the work I do. I hoped that I would be able to inspire her to see that by taking little steps, you can make it from hiding outside the door to entering the room, and then eventually being on the stage, if you want to.

Knowing why you're doing it helps you to overcome the fear and the sweat and the very strong desire you may have to run for the hills.

Because if you don't do it, then who will? And how will you have an impact, help your people, fulfil your mission or purpose? It's hard to do that from under a blanket. Or when you're peering in through a window covered in old pieces of chewing gum.

Shy allies assemble

I am really a loner, after all; I am really not a social person . . .
Because of my job, people think I am out every night, but I really
hate all that. I am somebody who likes to be alone and see some close
friends. I am a shy and introspective person.

Tom Ford, fashion designer

One of the most brilliant things about the internet is that it enables us to connect with people who are just like us. The fact that shy people can choose to come and hang out with me in the Shy and Mighty Society strikes me as completely marvellous. Yeah, it's possibly the quietest place on the internet – but that's what makes it special. We are supremely lucky. A quick google and you can pretty much find your kind of gang, no matter where you live on this planet. You don't even need to leave the house to chat to them.

If you're spending time with people who talk over you, who don't value your opinion, who don't listen to you, who drain you of every last iota of energy, stop.

If you're hanging out with people who don't make you happy, stop. Disentangle yourself.

I'm not saying you need to cut people out of your life altogether. Or cancel anyone. Or make some kind of radical public announcement denouncing the people in your life who've annoyed you in some way. Just that you might want to slide a little more towards being around a small handful of people who light you up. Shy allies.

Don't let teams just happen around you. Build your team intentionally. Be a quietly confident, shy and mighty leader.

Start small. Even if your community is more of a tiny huddle, that's ok. Starting with a small, perfectly formed gang of two or three is easier to handle than an unwieldy committee. Pick one or two key people to come on board and get the ball rolling.

Being part of a team is heavenly, if you're in the right team! I've been in more than one healthy, collaborative team — one for five years. I'm at peak performance and joy under those conditions.

Georgia

Choose positive people who lift you up and make you feel good. That doesn't mean you have to surround yourself with people who agree with everything you say. That would be weird.

Have you heard the people plumbing adage?

Some people are radiators. They are warm. They radiate energy and positivity. They're enthusiastic and upbeat, fun to be around and they warm your bottom if you lean on them. Some people are drains. They drain you of energy. They are negative and whiney, suck all the fun out of life and are exhausting to be around. Sometimes they need unblocking, but you definitely don't want to be around for that.

Choose to be a radiator. And to surround yourself with radiators too.

Choose people with complementary skills, and knowledge to plug any gaps in your own. And track down people with skills and talents that are important to you. Things like thinking deeply and listening, perhaps? But resist the temptation to select loud, dominant people in the hope that you can hide behind them, as you'll end up fading away into the background. I've done that before.

When you're pushing yourself forwards, striving to achieve big things, not everyone will want to accompany you on your journey. People don't like change, and when they see you changing it may make them feel threatened. That's ok. You can't force people to understand that you're on a road to becoming more mighty.

The sad truth is that you might not get unwavering, solid support from family and friends. But, if you can, avoid the naysayers, disbelievers, downers and downright toxic people. You can choose who to let into your inner circle.

Fighting is a solitary sport, yet boxers are not alone. In the gym, they have coaches, nutritionists, and of course their sparring partners and gym buddies. During the fight itself, every boxer has a corner team. There's someone to wipe away their sweat and blood. Someone to give them water. Someone to patch them up with that weird Vaseline goop. Someone to have a strong word with them. In their toughest moments, when a three-minute round feels like an eternity, they are pushing themselves to the extreme and every muscle and sinew in their bodies wants to go home for a nap, they are definitely not alone.

Coaching is not just for sport. Having someone in your corner who understands you, challenges you and holds you accountable can help you achieve more than you ever thought possible. Someone who can see things objectively and knows your true capabilities helps you to become more mighty. As a boxer myself, I know there have been moments when I really wanted to give up and go home. But I didn't – because my coach, Brian, helped me find that last bit of grit and strength.

We all need people in our corner.

Ask for help

Amika George set up 'Free Periods', a campaign to destroy period poverty, when she was a teenager. When she discovered that 10 per cent of girls in the UK don't have the money to purchase period products, Amika decided to take action, but she couldn't do it alone.

She set up an online petition, collected thousands of signatures, staged a massive peaceful protest outside Downing Street and even took legal action against the government. What a woman. Eventually, the government took notice, and from 2019, period products were offered for free in all secondary schools and colleges in England. Wow.

I'm bad at bookkeeping, awful at accounting, pretty poor at doing my own PR. And I'm ok with that. I also know that there are plenty of things that I may not be awful at, but other people can do better than me. So, instead of battling on with all these things, I get help. I don't see it as an admission of failure. In fact, to me, it seems smart.

Trying to manage on your own at work or at home will leave you frazzled. Soldiering on, dealing with all aspects of your shyness by yourself is tricky. And completely unnecessary. Refusing to get help may feel like a show of strength. In fact, it's a big mistake.

I get that letting go and getting help can be scary. I used to worry that people wouldn't understand, or they would judge me, or that, by asking for help, I was letting myself down. I know that it can feel like you're being a nuisance. You don't want to be a pain. It can make you feel defensive. Like you are opening yourself up to criticism.

But asking for help is not a sign of weakness. As someone who is shy and mighty, you don't need to do everything alone.

If you don't have the skills to build a company, get your dream job or enter a new field, then go and acquire them through schooling, a mentor, online courses, seminars or reading.

You can only grow so far on your own. An expert team is necessary to support big-time growth.

Logan Chierotti, entrepreneur*

So, ask a buddy to help you with your presentation, accompany you to an event, stand up with you on stage, introduce you to the person you've been eyeing up at the bar. Or simply talk about your shy feelings with a friend when they pop up. With a supporter by your side, being mighty is much easier.

And, if you struggle to ask for help, think about the other person. Helping others is a nice thing to do. It feels good to help. So, why deprive someone of that nice, fuzzy feeling?

---

* https://www.growwire.com/logan-chierotti

SHY POINTS

- We shy people have the potential to achieve big things.
- But we need to be in the arena to be in with a chance of success.
- By embracing collaboration and community, we can become mighty, together.

CHAPTER 10

SHY SCREAM

I was the shyest human ever invented, but I had a lion inside me that wouldn't shut up.

Ingrid Bergman, actor

Rhia had been feeling out of sorts for a few days. She had an atrocious pain in her stomach, and she just couldn't shift it.

She called the doctor's surgery, but they told her there were no appointments available for three weeks. Not wanting to make a fuss, she decided to see if it would right itself after a few days. Eventually, the pain became so intense that she collapsed at work. Her boss insisted that she go to the hospital to get it checked. She waited around on her own, for seven hours or so, sitting quietly in the waiting room. She didn't complain or pester the nurses, because she didn't want to inconvenience anyone. She figured she'd call her husband when she had some news because there was no point worrying him as he was away on business.

The doctors examined Rhia but couldn't find anything conclusive. They did an ultrasound to check her appendix, but they couldn't see it.

They asked her when she'd had her appendix taken out, and when they suggested she must have had it removed when she was a kid, because she was feeling so frail and befuddled, she didn't really have the heart to disagree.

There was a shortage of beds, so Rhia was told to wait in the corridor on a trolley until someone came for her. Nobody came. She was there for a long time, by herself, drifting in and out of sleep. A day or so passed, and still Rhia didn't want to make a fuss. Friends were texting, but she didn't really know what to say. She didn't want to worry them, so she didn't reply.

When her husband, who was working abroad in South Africa, didn't hear from Rhia for a couple of days, he got worried. He called around trying to track her down, but nobody seemed to know where she was. He called her office and found out what had happened, and when he realised that she hadn't been seen since, he freaked out, jumped on a plane and raced home.

When he arrived at the hospital, he tracked Rhia down and found her at death's door. He could not believe what he was seeing. His wife was barely recognisable. She was slipping away. He shouted and screamed and grabbed the doctors. He advocated for her, very, very loudly.

It turned out that Rhia did have an appendix, but it had burst when she collapsed at work, and she had been being poisoned from the inside ever since.

She was dying quietly in the corridor, too weak and meek to make a fuss. She had silently slipped through the cracks.

Rhia was rushed into surgery and luckily, in the nick of time, she was saved.

We shy people have a tendency to fall silent when it really matters.

In moments of stress and danger, our amygdala kicks into action and, as we saw earlier (see pp. 90–92), starts sending blood to our legs and arms, so we can fight the baddies we are facing. It diverts attention away from our mouth and throat and jaw, so we can't stuff doughnuts into our faces or sit around chatting when we should be lion fighting. Fair enough, Aunt Amy – that is helpful.

Shy people are dominated by feelings of fear and worry and awkwardness. These can feel so insurmountable that some of us would rather die silently on a trolley than draw attention to ourselves or risk a confrontation.

Don't make a scene

Leonie smelled. Everyone at school said so. They chanted it at playtime. They wrote notes about it. They whispered it.

I liked Leonie. We weren't best mates or anything, but she was nice. And I am 100 per cent certain that Leonie did not smell.

For a good couple of years, I would think this to myself on a daily basis. Leonie doesn't smell. Why are they saying that? But I never spoke up or said anything. And to this day, I feel so bad about the fact that I didn't want to rock the boat or take a stand.

I was too afraid to be the next one who was accused of smelling, or looking funny, or most likely, sounding funny. I didn't speak up. In the face of massive injustice, I did nothing. I stayed silent. The social threat was too scary. Saying nothing was safer. For me. But not for Leonie.

Why do we say nothing? Because we're afraid of upsetting people. Of confrontation. Of dealing with awkwardness and discomfort.

When I spot confrontation, I run a mile. I don't like it. Never have. (Bit strange for a boxer, but hey.) Even writing about it makes me squirm. I would rather do anything else than have to have a difficult conversation.

Our old neighbours used to shout and yell at each other. Their screaming was so loud and intense, you couldn't really tell who was shouting at who. But the way they spoke to each other was shocking. She was pregnant. I was worried about the baby. It put me on edge, and even with a 120-year-old wall separating our two houses, it felt too close for comfort. It's hard to relax watching TV when you're worried about a blood bath next door.

I wanted to say something. We would bump into each other in the street, and I would want to let her know we could hear them, to see if she was ok. But I didn't.

In the end, to avoid an awkward conversation, we moved house.

In the style of Homer Simpson, I would much rather simply disappear backwards into a hedge. I would rather vanish than have to handle this stuff.

One boiling hot summer, when I was a teenager, I worked in a very sweaty pub kitchen. The owner of the pub was a total perv and would make inappropriate comments and rub up against the girls when he walked past.

Even though it made me feel uncomfortable, I didn't want to make a scene. I didn't say anything, let alone knee him in the nuts. I was a good girl.

There have been so many times that I've said nothing: times when I didn't agree with what was being said, times when I wanted to stand up for myself, or put myself forward, or express my opinions or wants and needs.

But I didn't.

Over time, silence builds. The less you speak up, the harder it becomes – you know how it is when you wake up in the morning, and because you've not said anything for ages, your voice comes out all hoarse and whispery when you do speak. It's like that.

We put our needs aside

People get my name wrong all the time. Nadine. Nardia. Natalie. I tell myself that I'm so used to people getting it wrong that that's why I don't say anything. But really, the truth is, I never say anything because it's awkward.

I know I should correct them the first time it happens.

But I don't. And the years go by. Now, saying something would be ridiculous. By the way, you've been saying my name wrong for the past seven years, only I was too embarrassed to tell you.

Last weekend, I was feeling really tired and overwhelmed by life. I'd had a couple of late nights, I'd been working hard, rushing around doing too many things. My body was telling me to rest up. I felt like I had nothing more to give.

All I wanted to do was snuggle up with my book, in silence, undisturbed for an hour or two. I had an actual longing to do that; a force was pulling me towards my book and my bed. I knew that if I could just manage to relax for a bit, I could emerge all springy and shiny back into the world.

But the messages kept pinging. People with their dramas. People needing help. My friend called. She wanted to talk. But the reception was bad, and her phone kept cutting out. I rang her back, about seven times. More messages. More reminders. Everyone wanted a piece of me, and all I wanted to do was read my bloody book. I actually felt despair, or like I might cry.

Did I tell anyone that? Did I explain that I wasn't in a position to help anyone right then, because I was tired and didn't have the headspace and I just needed a moment?

Of course I didn't.

I don't mind. It's fine. Whatever you want is fine by me. Whatever you want to say is fine by me. Whatever you want to do to me is fine by me. But is it?

Living our lives like a doormat, too afraid to speak up? That's no way to live.

When you're silent you miss out

Keeping quiet is easier in the moment. Nobody is offended. Nobody is upset. Nobody has to change what they're doing.

But longer term, it's frustrating and infuriating. Silence leads to regrets. You can't get involved, or say yes, or say no, when you're silent. You're more likely to be overlooked or underestimated. You're more likely to miss out.

Yes, you have a rich and fascinating dialogue going on in your head, but you're not interacting with other people. Your thoughts and ideas and opinions never see the light of day.

When you're silent, you don't experience life fully. You're not interacting or making friends or joining in the conversation. You're not having new experiences or having fun. You're lurking in the shadows, like a ghost.

Speaking up at school

You want to put your hand up because you've got something to say, but the thought of thirty sets of eyes on you scares you. You're worried that you might mess up or make a mistake. You remember the time you said something, and everyone laughed at you.

So you keep quiet.

It's frustrating because you're bursting with ideas, and you want so much to speak up. But staying silent is less complicated.

Every time a teacher asks a question in a lesson, and I know the answer, I don't contribute. Every parents' evening, they tell me to actively participate more. Like, I'd love to! You saying that won't change anything, though, as it's not my fault.

Smith

Speaking up socially

I don't fall out with people. Mainly because I never tell them they've upset me.

I've put up with all kinds of nonsense, judgements and strange behaviour from people who are meant to be my friends. And I've avoided telling them how I feel because I couldn't face the awkwardness of the confrontation.

I have no issue advocating and speaking up for my patients or colleagues at work, but find it difficult socially and feel talked over by those more outgoing, which takes me further into myself. Often, I feel I have nothing interesting to say.

Mason

Speaking up in relationships

Staying silent in a relationship is not just awkward, it can be dangerous. Take my friend Carrie.

The first time he was rough with her, she didn't speak up. She thought it was less than ideal, but she brushed it under the carpet. She didn't want to upset him. She didn't want to make a fuss. So, she just went along with it. She had doubts and a little voice in her head telling her to leave, but she didn't.

As the months went by, she was belittled and berated. The grip had tightened on her throat. Until speaking to anyone became impossible.

Have you ever stuck around longer than you should have? Have you kept your needs to yourself? Have you silenced the voices in your head telling you to speak up for yourself?

Staying silent starts small. But it builds and builds until speaking up becomes impossible.

If you silence your own needs for long enough, eventually you won't even know what you want any more.

I often did not speak up in my marriage, but now I am an older woman and I have a lot to feel angry about, I am speaking up more and more. But it has caused a huge rift between us! I guess my husband has had years of not realising how unhappy he made me. I have suffered in silence. I was not strong enough for my kids. A lot of stuff has happened over the years which I now feel guilty for as I did not stand up to him or speak out.

Velda

Speaking up at work

Speaking up and showing up at work can be hard, particularly when you're a shy person, and your workplace feels like a coliseum packed to the nines with a baying crowd, with you the newbie gladiator, fighting for survival.

Most organisations don't have a culture of listening or nurturing quieter voices. We often feel underqualified for the work we are doing and are afraid to rock the boat or challenge people in senior positions. In workplaces where hierarchy is steep and bosses are dominant, for personalities who don't like being questioned or criticised, speaking up can feel like a futile exercise.

As a result, quieter voices are silenced. Ideas are hidden. Solutions are not shared.

When I got my first job as a graduate, I was told that I needed to raise my profile, but I had no idea how to do that. If I'm honest, I didn't really know what they meant. I knew I was good at what I did, so why did I have to shout about it and big myself up? Surely people would notice me because of the work I did?

Except it didn't really work like that. I noticed that some people seemed to know how to play the game. They would get great opportunities and take credit for things they hadn't done. They had a knack for speaking up with confidence just at the right moment, even if they didn't actually add anything to the substance of the conversation.

And my silence was deafening.

I was afraid of speaking up when somebody made a racist remark towards me. It was the first time someone had ever done that to me, and it happened at work. I was shocked and just stayed quiet. I beat myself up about it later because I felt I didn't uphold my values and true character. I was scared this person would influence my future job offers and everybody else would think I was being dramatic because I was known to be pleasant and quiet. It would have been a big flip from being the quiet employee to an argumentative one. I was also relatively new and just starting to get used to the environment. I

was afraid I'd say something to make the conflict worse and nobody
would support me. This experience is what made me realise my shyness
needed to improve. If not for my own sake, for the sake of others who
have to deal with things like this.

Selma

I remember the day our new boss, Paul, arrived on the scene. It was like a takeover. He was a huge alpha male in an office of quiet women. Over the weeks that followed, I noticed that people were being replaced, one by one, as he proceeded to bring in all his chums from his old place of work. It was a strange experience, turning up to work each day to find yet another hardworking woman had been replaced by a large, arrogant dude. It was as if the clock had struck midnight and they were being cloned, one suit at a time.

The whole vibe of the place changed so subtly that I wondered if I was imagining things. Until one day, in a meeting, I realised we were surrounded by a whole gang of Pauls. They even joked that the gang was back together.

Paul was happy. I wasn't. I left shortly after that.

Let's say Paul was great at his job. It doesn't seem too strange that he'd look for another Paul. But a whole company of Pauls? That's a lotta Pauls. And a lot of balding middle-aged men who all went to the same university, support the same sports team, live in the same area, in the same kind of houses, do the same kind of jobs, earn the same amount of money, and have the same political opinions. Same, same, same, same.

It's human nature to be attracted to people like us. When we build teams or recruit, there's a tendency to go for those people. It's called homophily. It may be conscious, or subconscious, but the upshot is, our entourage ends up consisting solely of people who are like us, and who are more likely to agree with us.

As a shy person, getting that big promotion or grabbing that spot on the board is not easy as it is. And because the people in positions of power, making the decisions and building the teams, are nothing like us, when it comes to recruiting in their own image, we don't match the photofit.

But does this carbon-copy clique get better results? Erm, no.

By surrounding yourself with a bunch of clones, you are weakening your team and your chances of success. When everyone thinks the same, says the same and does the same, things get missed.

It's the reason Matthew Syed argues in his book, *Rebel Ideas*, that Osama bin Laden was able to orchestrate the 9/11 terror attacks.

The CIA was jam-packed with white men from middle- and upper-class backgrounds who had mostly studied the same sort of arts subjects at university. Sure, they were well educated, but they were too alike. They had experienced similar things, lived in the same kind of areas, met the same kind of people, worked in the same kind of jobs. They had a similar outlook on life.

Without knowing it, they had become what Syed calls 'collectively blind'.

And because of that, they failed to detect important clues about Osama bin Laden. Their knowledge of Islam was extremely limited. They catastrophically underestimated him. Their prejudices blinded them. And they never considered that some bedraggled, grubby guy who lived in a cave could be capable of masterminding an atrocity that killed thousands of people.

In my job, I used to support a girl who rarely spoke. I could empathise with her, and she actually used to speak to me. In one meeting about her with other staff, I tried to explain this feeling of knowing what to say but being unable to speak, of feeling physically incapable of voicing it. I asked if anyone else had ever had that experience. Not one other person had.

Blondene

It's hard to question things when you're worried about being a lone voice of dissent.

But it is possible for everyone to just be nodding and slapping each other on the back and not really thinking logically.

Imagine being the only native English speaker in an international product team. Imagine sitting in a meeting where the wording on a shower-gel bottle label that made absolutely no sense in English was being signed off. Imagine mentioning this quietly, only to be told that you were wrong.

I knew their decision was insane, and I also knew that in that moment they didn't want to be told they were wrong. They didn't want to listen, and I didn't want to rock the boat. So, I took a deep breath and said nothing. I succumbed to the pressure to conform.

Afterwards, I spoke to one of my teammates quietly, and it turns out that they too had doubts. But neither of us had said anything.

This problem is called the Abilene paradox. It is what happens when a bunch of people make a decision that goes against their individual better judgement. It happens when each person thinks that they are the only one who disagrees and decides to say nothing.

But if we're scared to speak up about the wording on a shower-gel label, what happens when we are faced with something more serious?

I had a Sunday job working in a deli kitchen. It was not clean at all. In fact, it was downright filthy.

I tried my best to clean it, but it didn't really make a dent. And when I noticed the mouse poo, my first thought was that I didn't want to get into trouble or lose my job. I didn't want to offend anyone. So, I said nothing.

In 1989, a Boeing 737 from London to Belfast had a fault in one of its engines. The captain announced over the loudspeaker that he had switched off the right-hand engine. The cabin crew and passengers could see that, in fact, it was the left-hand engine that was engulfed in a ball of flames. The captain had turned off the wrong engine. The plane was now entirely without engines.

But nobody spoke up. The cabin crew knew better than to interrupt or criticise the captain. The passengers could see the fire on the left-hand side of the plane, but they presumed the captain knew what he was doing.

The plane crashed short of the runway, smashing into the side of the M1 motorway. Forty-seven people died.

Analysis of black-box recordings have found that failure to challenge authority is a major issue in the aviation industry. Junior crew members or co-pilots find it hard to speak up, particularly in moments of crisis, and if they do, they aren't direct enough, which leads to their input being ignored.

Doctors need to be able to communicate well as a team, particularly in an emergency, but they also need the skills and confidence to be able to challenge authority. Creating a culture of speaking up, and psychological safety at work, is crucial in hospitals, if cases like that of Elaine Bromley are to be avoided.

Elaine was a healthy young woman who was struggling to breathe. Two experienced consultant anaesthetists and an ear, nose and throat surgeon tried and tried to help her breathe. As the level of panic in the room rose, the nurses could see how critical the situation was becoming. They realised a tracheostomy was the only way to help her breathe, but even though they brought the equipment into the room, they didn't suggest it. Those nurses tried to hint that something was wrong, while avoiding criticising the senior staff. It wasn't enough. Elaine died.

On another occasion, a surgical team were preparing a young child for surgery. A junior doctor in the room noticed they were prepping the wrong hand. She tried to alert them to the mistake, but she was ignored. She tried again to inform them that they were making a mistake, but they got cross and told her to pipe down. The operation went ahead – on the wrong hand.

Speaking up is tricky, particularly when you're a junior with limited power at the bottom of the hierarchical pile. You might feel intimidated because you're not as skilled or experienced, or maybe you're a quiet voice in a room filled with loud ones.

Nowadays, the airline industry is leading the way, creating a culture where it is safe to speak up. And because there are similar structures of hierarchy in the NHS, they're sharing their expertise with medical teams.

Pilots and co-pilots are now trained to communicate clearly using unambiguous language. They're taught to use specific trigger phrases, like 'I am concerned', 'I am uncomfortable', 'This is unsafe' and 'We need to stop'. They're encouraged to report their mistakes, welcome feedback and be more assertive.

Making shyness work for us at work

I find it tricky to fit my views in when there is an overpowering, loud presence. I kind of shrink a bit more. I think it would be a start if more people recognised that it's ok to be shy . . . and not calling people out on being shy would be great too . . . people find the need to tell me I'm quiet, whereas I'm not sure they would say to someone, 'God you're really gobby, aren't you?' I think it makes others feel uneasy.

Kristal

This stuff is hugely important for the future of work, society and the world as we know it. Just saying.

Badly run meetings that are dominated by individuals or their agendas; I encounter this a lot working in government, which, despite purporting to be inclusive, can be driven by some weighty topics where individual feelings can be lost. I recently experienced the opposite, where the chair began by saying, 'Let's all check in with how we are feeling'. It felt wonderfully empowering.

Ash

If you'd like me to come and chat to your organisation about becoming more shy-person friendly, and maybe kick their butts a little to ensure that all voices are heard, ping me a message and I'll be there!

Stranger than fiction

I've been binge-watching the French police drama, *Spiral*, or, in French, the much cooler word 'Engrenages', meaning gears. It's gritty, gripping, and, erm, pretty gruesome, to be honest. I have to spend roughly 10 per cent of each episode looking away. And I wouldn't recommend eating your dinner while watching.

In one episode, a witness to a murder was shy, or *timide*. The barrister was yelling at her to stop being so shy. And the more she was shouting at her, the more this woman shrunk down, unable to speak.

She was the only witness to a murder. Her testimony was crucial to convicting the murderer. It struck me that if we shy people are unable to speak up, say, in the courtroom, there could be serious consequences. The trial process plays out like a drama, with an audience and so much pressure. It's yet another situation not designed for shy people to shine.

And it turns out, this is not just the stuff of fiction. A Sydney jury heard that a young girl was abused by her swimming teacher over the course of many months, but had been too shy to tell anyone or say anything.

'I was too shy to tell him to stop and I was too shy to tell my mother and father. I just didn't want to talk about it,' she said. *

---

* https://www.canberratimes.com.au/story/7010569/girl-too-shy-to-talk-about-swim-teacher/?cs=14231

Society, and its structures have not been designed for us shy people. We are living in a world not made for us. And I think it's time we all did something about it.

What if we talked about shyness in meetings? What if we looked out for the signs that someone was struggling? What if we asked if they needed support, rather than dismissing them as lazy or arrogant? What if we encouraged ideas to be shared prior to meetings? What if we recruited a range of voices? What if we offered mentoring and support more widely? What if we designed offices with areas for quiet reflection? What if meetings were structured to encourage sharing and collaboration? What if we encouraged creativity and experimentation? What if we made it safe to experiment and make mistakes? What if we allowed people time and space to speak uninterrupted? What if we gave people the opportunity to share ideas without fear of judgement?

What if shyness was something we talked about and considered when teams are created, meetings held, people recruited, buildings designed, justice done, politics played out?

When quieter voices are missing from the conversation, we all miss out. So, let's all make it safe for shy people to speak up.

We need a range of voices

The current discussion around diversity and inclusion has focused on demographics, gender, skin colour, social mobility and education. But what about the way we think? What about our behavioural preferences? What about the way we show up in the world? Diversity is surely about making sure everyone is represented; everyone is heard.

We need a mixture of personalities, perspectives and skills to function.

If shy people don't speak up and are under-represented in meetings, hospitals, cockpits, classrooms, in society, the only voices we hear are the loud ones.

To solve the trickiest problems and generate the best ideas, organisations and teams need a mixture of personalities and preferences. They need cognitive diversity to function and succeed and innovate, particularly in challenging times.

If you bring together people who think in different ways, whose brains work differently, *you're* more likely to think differently, to use varied approaches, ask challenging questions, solve difficult problems and come up with creative solutions. You're less likely to miss things. Your team will have mighty powers.

Medical company 3M were trying to figure out how to reduce the risk of patients being exposed to infection during surgery. To work on the challenge, they embraced cognitive diversity. They assembled a team of experts with different backgrounds: a veterinary surgeon, a wound-healing expert and, most awesomely, a theatrical make-up expert. Together, in the style of a superhero team, they invented a completely unique product that met their needs. It makes sense that having people with different skills and experiences leads to innovative results.

The lack of shy role models and the fact that we don't talk about shyness means that we are not part of the conversation. We are not represented. Which makes it even harder for us to speak up.

We need to change that. And we need to show up in our own way. Sure, we are surrounded by people shouting all the time, but that doesn't mean we should shout too. That's not us, and that's not what the world needs.

We need shy voices. To share ideas, to solve problems, to notice when things are not working, to improve situations, to draw attention to wrongdoings. We need shy voices to change the world.

SHY POINTS

- Fear, worry and awkwardness can be stronger than our desire to speak up.
- We struggle to speak up in the face of authority at school, socially and at work.
- Diversity is about making sure everyone is represented; everyone is heard.
- Society is not designed to amplify quieter voices.
- When quieter voices are missing from the conversation, we all miss out.

SHY POWER

SHY POWER: HOW TO BECOME SHY AND MIGHTY

- Mighty Me: Own your shyness. Don't shy away from it.
- Mighty Free: Care carefully. Let go of judgement.
- Mighty Snug: Comfort, kindness and safety help us to become mighty.
- Mighty Fight: Tap into your inner strength and develop your mighty mindset.
- Mighty Powers: You are not broken. You have super skills.
- Mighty Muscles: From invisible to invincible, one mighty move at a time.

CHAPTER 11

MIGHTY ME

The whole, like, sensitive, fragile thing. I do have those qualities,
and I just don't think there's anything wrong with them.

Winona Ryder, actor*

I was about to stride onto the stage and face an audience of hundreds. My nerves were jangling like an array of heavy gold gangsta chains around my neck, weighing me down. And that's when my colleague stepped in, with these pearls of wisdom: *'Don't be so shy. Whatever you do, don't let on how you feel.'*

The direction was crystal clear: hide your shyness, slap a smile on your face and get on with it. I may as well have had someone in the wings giving me a powerful shove out of my comfort zone and onto the stage. In fact, I'm pretty sure I had had just that.

How the hell was I going to hide how I was really feeling? My voice, tiny at the best of times, was shaky, my cheeks were flushed and I was certain that my heart was visibly pounding out of my chest. No doubt about it, people would be able to see my dirty little secret.

---

* Heather Havrilesky, 'Winona Uninterrupted', *New York Magazine*, 8 August 2016.

I could have tried to fake it, but pretending is exhausting, and I'm not a convincing actor; my superficial smile would have been more of a grimace. I do not have a poker face, I have a flushed, twitchy face – one that cannot maintain eye contact.

But, you know, there is something about his words that still rankles me to this day. '*Don't be so shy.*'

Yes, I'm shy, but I also don't like being told what to do. All this fakery and pretending doesn't sit well with me. Maybe deep down I'm lazy, but it feels like a lot of effort. And frankly, why should I have to pretend? When someone tells me to stop being so shy, it feels like they're telling me to change who I am.

It's not that easy. The idea that someone tells me to stop being shy so I simply flick the shy switch and, ta-da, I'm magically transformed into a whole new person, doesn't work. In fact, attempting to mask my shyness has had a rather embarrassing and completely uncontrollable consequence in the past.

When I was a kid, I was at a family event. For some reason, I had been asked to make a little speech. How and why someone decided that I would be a good person for that particular job makes me question pretty much everything. But there I was, standing, quivering, in front of family and friends, trying to pretend to be fine with public speaking. And that's when my attempts at masking my shyness completely backfired.

I was seized by the giggles.

I couldn't stop. I just stood there laughing uncontrollably, like I had been possessed. It was mortifying. I ended up having to be shuffled off the stage. I can't remember what happened after that. Perhaps they had to sedate me, who knows.

Anyway, fast-forward back to the moment when I was about to step out onto the stage, as an adult.

The quiet, reserved rebel inside me dug her heels in.

I was not going to pretend. I took the mic and I decided that I would tell people that I was feeling really nervous and shy. I decided to just get it out into the open, so I could get on with my talk and not worry that I would somehow get found out.

I dragged my gaze up, from my shoes, and, you know, people weren't laughing at me. They were smiling. I could feel their warmth, radiating out towards me. They wanted me to do well. They were on my side. And that's when I knew that I could be mighty, just the way I am.

Given that around half of humans are shy, as we know, and pretty much everyone, aside from a few psychopaths (joking, well, sort of), have experienced shyness at some point in their lives, that means that people understand. They've been there. They know what it's like.

There's strength in our shyness.

When I was at school, we used to get reports each year with marks per subject, plus comments from each teacher. Our form teacher would add some pithy comments at the bottom. We all thought it was funny that he would try to summarise us in two or three words. His comment for me was 'quiet power'. It has always stayed in my mind.

My dad, Steve

My dad is the epitome of shy power. He doesn't shout or scream. He doesn't bully people. Or talk over them. Or dismiss their ideas. He's calm under pressure. He respects people and listens to them. He believes in what he does and works hard to achieve his goals. He leads by example and motivates and inspires others to do their best. Quietly. He's shy and he's mighty.

When we own our shyness and find the courage to speak up, we bring shyness into the open and people understand that they're not the only ones who feel like this.

I spent so many years of my life hiding, because of my little voice, feeling so self-conscious and embarrassed about the way I sound. But I've come to realise that there's strength in my shyness; there's mightiness in my little voice. When I speak, people lean in and listen. When I speak, they stop what they are doing and pay attention. My voice is instantly recognisable. My voice is memorable.

Gosh, it makes me feel weird to write that. It's funny how something I was so ashamed of has become a sort of superpower.

It's ok to open up and be vulnerable

Being vulnerable, open and honest is a sign of bravery, not weakness. I'm not advocating the faux vulnerability that celebs seem to whip out willy nilly; that's just fake and gross. But, if you are feeling shy, it's ok to talk about it and bring it out of the shadows without shame or fear of judgement.

> *Vulnerability is not winning or losing; it's having the courage to show up and be seen when we have no control over the outcome. Vulnerability is not weakness; it's our greatest measure of courage.*
>
> Brené Brown, *Rising Strong*

I believe there's a beautiful truth to talking about shyness. The very act of opening up about it involves overcoming it. Pow!

There's a raw quality to shyness. It's a normal human reaction, which most people, if they are being honest, understand.

Over the years, I've been drawn to the music of the singer-songwriter Nick Drake. From the South of France to the Five Ways roundabout in Birmingham, my life has crossed the faint shadow of his path many times. His voice was unsteady, vulnerable and raw, with so much richness that it could melt even the iciest of hearts. Nick Drake was incredibly shy, and during his very short life, was loath to perform live or be interviewed. As a result, despite signing to Island Records, he was not particularly famous or successful in his lifetime. He lamented the fact that his art wasn't appreciated and predicted that only once he was long gone would people really see his genius.

> Fame is but a fruit tree, so very unsound. It can never flourish,
> 'til its stock is in the ground. So men of fame, can never find a
> way, 'til time has flown, far from their dying day.*

But his legacy lives on. Why? Because his music resonates and moves us. There is so much emotion in his soft, buttery voice and heart-breaking authenticity in the stories he tells.

Fame is fine. But unveiling your true voice and having the courage to open up and speak to people about the things that really matter to you, now that's important.

And if you happen to speak your truth in a soft, beautiful way, that gives people the tingles, even better.

---

* Nick Drake, 'Fruit Tree', produced by Joe Boyd and Robert Kirby, 3 July 1969.

Soft is strong

Nick Drake is proof that softly spoken is powerful.

If you have a quieter voice, people might talk over you, you might have to repeat yourself over and over, or actually bellow in someone's ear to be heard. It can make you waver and falter, and question whether the effort of being heard is even worth it. And yes, the less you talk, the harder it is to talk, like your voice thinks it's 6am and you've just woken up. And yes, when you feel like everyone is looking at you, your throat constricts and the words just don't seem to want to come out.

I've learned to love my little voice. Having spent most of my life shying away from the way I sound, nowadays I'm a fan of quiet voices. Speaking, or singing, softly is comforting, and calming. Parents speak softly to their babies for a reason, after all. We're not likely to cause headaches. Or get on people's nerves. And actually, quiet voices can be damn sexy.

Shyness as a label

I didn't set out to be at the top of technology companies. I'm just geeky and shy and I like to code.

Marissa Mayer, businesswoman and investor*

Some people reckon that, by admitting to being shy, you're writing it in permanent marker on your forehead. They worry that calling yourself shy means you'll end up living out the story you're telling yourself. They believe that labelling ourselves as shy leads us to behave more shyly.

---

* https://matterapp.com/blog/introvert-leaders-can-remain-introverts-and-still-crush-it-2/

Labelling ourselves as anything can be problematic. Having a label can feel limiting, like we've put ourselves in a box and closed the lid. This is particularly true if that label has toxic levels of shame and stigma associated with it.

We don't want to give ourselves an excuse to hide or avoid speaking up, or give others a reason to speak on our behalf. We don't want to get stuck in a self-fulfilling prophecy.

But, ignoring our shyness, masking over it, hiding away from it, is also not particularly healthy.

How about, rather than labelling ourselves as shy, and making ourselves feel like even more of an outcast, we acknowledge our emotions, and make friends with our shyness. Because, ultimately, learning to love all the different parts of ourselves, and all the different things we feel, is a good thing.

Humans have a whole array of emotions and feelings. We change and develop throughout our lifetime. And, like a river, or your love of punk rock, your shyness may ebb and flow in and out of your life. We are not stuck in a sticky bog, rooted to the spot.

When we own our shyness, and understand it better, we can figure out how to work with it, and make it work for us. Acknowledging our shyness doesn't mean we are stuck in stasis. It's the first step in taking action and moving forwards, out of the shadows and into a bigger life.

Shyness is a mirror

I find eye contact extremely difficult. I was on a placement and my boss called me into his office and said he was going to help me practise eye contact. He put a sticker between his eyes and said I had to hold eye contact for five minutes. It was absolutely horrendous. I felt if I didn't do it, I would get fired. I felt sick. But I couldn't do it and I refused. I left the room and cried.

Sunita

Why are people so triggered by shyness? Why does shyness seem to aggravate people?

Maybe I got out of the wrong side of bed today, but I'm becoming awfully irritated by the way shyness is perceived. I'm fed up with bossy people telling me to get a grip, or yelling at me to be more confident, or to stop being so shy.

Perhaps, because we don't fit the mould, people want to morph us into something more palatable, easy to handle and understand. But I wonder if it's because our shyness holds a mirror up to their own true nature. Perhaps, beneath the mask of conviction superglued to their faces, they too are shy.

In any other situation, it would *NOT* be acceptable to bully someone into changing. And yet, with shyness it seems to be fair game. It's not on.

Hiding our true selves

Hedonism was like a disguise. I was a shy kid and I had to alter my personality. At first, it's freeing, but then it becomes a prison of its own making.

Florence Welch, musician*

* https://www.femalefirst.co.uk/music/musicnews/florence-welch-hedonism-disguise-shyness-1062669.html

We shy people don't like being looked at because it makes us feel self-conscious, embarrassed and uncomfortable. Many of us mask our shyness so that we can get on with our lives. We'll mask up and pretend to be something we're not, and nobody will have a clue what we're really feeling.

Given that we've lived through the Covid-19 pandemic, we've all experienced wearing a mask. We know what it's like to have a physical barrier between us and other humans. We know how it feels to hide our faces and feel anonymous. We know how masks hinder communication, muffle our already quiet voices, limit our vision and give us fierce acne.

When we cover who we really are and slap on a plastic persona, we present a version of ourselves to the world which we believe people will prefer.

I'm not the only one. On Instagram, you don't need to dig very deep to see the accounts that reveal the tricks and techniques people use in their photography. I've become addicted to those posts. I love seeing how on the same day someone can look six months pregnant or have washboard abs, just by adjusting their shorts a bit!

Hiding behind the filter protects us from judgement. It's another kind of mask, airbrushing away our uniqueness, and morphing us into one homogenised version of a human.

One size does not fit all

I'm not the girl at the club on the table. I'm going to be the one in the corner, quiet, so I don't call attention to myself. . . . I was the girl who cut school to go to the park, and the other kids would be smoking and drinking and I'd be reading Shakespeare.

Jessica Chastain, actor*

I can't jog. I hate it. It's boring. And painful. I don't want to do it. And yet, where I live jogging is the thing that everyone does.

For ages, I felt like I was a failure, like there was something wrong with me. But then I remembered that I've never been a long-distance runner.

I'm a sprinter. You can't beat the exhilaration of running full power. Back in the day, I was good at it. And in my head, I still am. Although I imagine I look more like Phoebe from *Friends* than Usain Bolt.

Turns out, there's a bit of science going on here. We are genetically disposed to have different types of muscles: slow-twitch and fast-twitch. Endurance athletes have more slow-twitch muscles and sprinters have more fast-twitch. That explains why my friend Claire can run and run and run without training; she can just start jogging and keep going Forrest-Gump style, for ever. I, on the other hand, cannot. I have fast-twitch muscles that are built for bursts of power. Explosive power. Which is, I think, why I can run fast, and punch as hard as a huge man.

You can train to improve your muscles, but you can't change your muscles from slow to fast or vice versa. And that goes for our

* https://highlysensitive.org/602/jessica-chastain-and-high-sensitivity/?fbclid=IwAR0_a7PVXLKEt38uXtuOIAVcT5pzVr6tH2OpD_-wn_GZWnMXzCfx71E8Ejs

personalities and behavioural preferences too. We can work on our skills, but we can't fundamentally change who we are. Nor should we. We can't all be the same. There isn't one version of a human. We are not clones. Or droids.

There's beauty and honesty and brilliance in our shyness. Why would we want to mask that? When we embrace who we are and we lean into it in all its sweaty glory, only then can we truly free ourselves from the shackles of shyness.

Comparisonitis kills confidence

Sarah was everything I was not. She could sing and dance. She loved the limelight. And the boys loved her. All through school and university she irritated the hell out of me. Looking at her was like looking in a distorted fairground mirror. Watching her do all the things I struggled with made me see my failings. And by spending too much time looking, I beat myself up constantly for being useless. Seeing her shine made me think that I wasn't shining at all.

It's human nature to compare ourselves with others. We like to check on other people, to check we are fitting in ok and to make sure we're not making a massive cock-up or social faux pas. When you think about it, that's why fashion is a thing. We follow trends so we blend in and conform, even if this season's silhouette makes us look ridiculous.

But sometimes our comparing can get out of hand, and instead of feeling reassured and comforted, we feel like we're not good enough, and comparisonitis slowly starts to eat away at our sense of self.

Writing this, I realise that I only compare myself with the loud, outgoing, über-confident, super-successful people. The queen bees,

The crème de la crème. I notice their Instagram feeds. Their gorgeous make-up and stylish outfits. Their luxury apartments. The way they can work out without pouring with sweat or ending up looking like they've been dragged through a hedge backwards. I compare myself with talk-show hosts. Champion boxers. International bestselling authors. Supermodels. I pick the top brass, compare myself with them, and when I'm not good enough, I feel all downhearted and dejected. Like I'm a total loser.

I don't go to a party and look for other quiet people and think, Oh look, that's my kind of person – maybe we should stand near each other and nod quietly at one another and prop up the bar in solidarity. Instead, I look at the most outgoing, exuberant people throwing shapes on the dance floor, shaking the things their mamas gave them. And I think. Oh lord. I can't do that. I am ridiculous and terrible and useless.

Comparing ourselves with chatty, outgoing people is compelling. They bring the fun, and we want it. They are desired and appreciated, surrounded by admirers. They reflect back at us all the things we are not. We feel we are not good enough, and that in order to be appreciated and loved we need to fundamentally change ourselves.

But spending our lives wishing we were different is a waste of a life.

Reframe the door

There's a brilliant quote by author and guru Joseph Campbell: 'The cave you fear to enter holds the treasure you seek'.

Our shyness is like a hidden doorway to greatness. We just need to find the courage to step over the threshold of the cave, to open the secret door. And once we do – once we're through the passageway – like Alice in Wonderland, we can access the magic.

We're lucky because not everyone has that secret door. But we do. We have all kinds of talents and gifts hidden behind this door. And there's something quite magical about that, don't you think?

Behind the door lie freedom of expression, honesty, vulnerability, true connection and inordinate amounts of potential. Behind the door lies our true power.

Rather than seeing our shyness as a block, or a barrier, or a prison, what if we see it as a magical door instead?

We are not just one thing

Like a delicious chocolate eclair, we are a beautiful mixture of layers. We are messy and talented. We are good at some things, and ridiculously bad at others. We are strong and kind, passionate and determined, silly and serious.

Our shyness is not all of us. It's just a part of who we are.

I'm shy. I'm brave. I'm a boxer. A writer.

Even if that person you envy is amazing at dancing and seems to lead a charmed existence, they have their mess and complexities. Nobody is perfect or happy all the time.

We might feel like we're not good enough. Like our thighs are too wobbly. Our voices are too quiet. Our faces are too wrinkly. Or spotty. Our hair isn't just so. Our skin is the wrong shade. We're too quiet. Too shy. Too much. Not enough.

Sometimes I'm shy and sometimes I'm loud. My shyness is just part of me.

You are shy and mighty.

MIGHTY MISSION

Try this to become instantly more mighty!

Own your shyness.

- Give your shyness a voice: drop it into the conversation, write about it, illustrate or sing about it – however you choose to express it. No more keeping your shyness secret and papering over it.

- Tune into your squirmy discomfort. Take a moment and breathe. Notice what's going on for you in your body and in your mind.

- Being honest with people is a brilliant thing. There's something so wonderful about having the courage to open up about how you really feel, rather than faking it and smashing through life as if everything is absolutely fine.

CHAPTER 12

MIGHTY FREE

I'd been so afraid of criticism ever since I was young. Every time I'd get a critique or some redirection, I'd always just take it very personally.

Jessica Alba, actor*

My first memory is the stuff of family legend.

When we were a mere eighteen months old, my twin brother, Ben, and I huddled together and hatched an ingenious plan. We decided to see what would happen if we yanked at the corner of the brand-new animal wallpaper freshly pasted on our walls.

We stood next to each other in our cot, partners in crime, ripping swathes of paper off the wall. It was excellent.

At around this age, tiny humans start to develop a sense of self, and recognise that we are independent of our parents. That was when I first revealed myself to be very quiet, but also a total menace.

When my parents discovered the havoc we had caused, they made it clear that destroying the house was unacceptable behaviour. So,

---

* https://popcrush.com/shy-celebrity-loners-introverts-gallery/

alongside my sense of self, I had also developed an understanding of the impact of my actions.

Don't judge me

When we go for a walk, and he's about to race off and explore, Bobby the dog always glances over his shoulder, hesitates for just a second and then, given the right words of encouragement, tears off into the distance. Adorable.

We humans also look outside ourselves for reassurance. We learn to base our decisions and feelings on the reactions of others. We learn to check in.

As kids, we check in with our parents. We soon realise that if we meet their expectations, say the right things, behave and dress the right way, we get praise, and maybe even some pocket money. And we check in with our friends, so we fit in. We make ourselves look attractive, but not too attractive. We make ourselves look cool, but not too cool. We try to become successful, but not too successful. Just enough, but not too much.

At school, we draw a picture, write an essay, produce a report, or create something truly splendid. And once it's done, we take a moment to bask in our glory: we gaze at the fruits of our labour, and revel in the sense of satisfaction and pride of a job well done. What a feeling!

And then we show it to someone else. We put our work out there to be judged. Will the teachers like it? Will it be what they were expecting? Will it be good enough? (But not too good, so that the other kids hate me?)

As adults, we put our work out into the world to be judged. And we ask the same questions.

Standing up, speaking up and standing out is so scary when you're shy. We don't want to draw attention to ourselves, but we crave praise and recognition. We feel pressure to show up and put ourselves out there, but the worries and anxieties that flood our shy brains are hard to handle. We get so caught up in the worries, caring so hard about what other people think. The judgements have taken over. It's paralysing.

This still makes me shudder and feel sick seven years on. It was my oldest friend's fiftieth birthday party. She's a photographer and has lots of actor and comedian friends. Midway through the party, her partner stopped the party and announced that I'd say a few words as an old mate. With no notice at all! Everything started to move very, very slowly. That room full of very confident people were all quiet and looking at me. I love my mate and we've had loads of fun adventures, but I could not think of one thing to say. I completely froze. I heard a woman (another bloody comedian) saying, 'Who's she? I should have done it.' I raised my glass, barely remembered my friend's name and slunk away to the toilet. The stuff of nightmares. We are still good friends and can laugh about it now, but it nearly finished me off!

Bea

Trying to please our parents, siblings, family, bosses, partners, friends. It's a lot. When the weight of these perceived judgements becomes so hefty, they pin us down – then there's a problem. We are permitting thoughts we cannot control, which are not based on truth, to govern our lives and cause us to miss out on opportunities, happiness, success and joy.

I fell in love with a musician. She was the one. But, my family and friends didn't approve. I couldn't handle the feeling that they were judging me. And I just couldn't escape the feeling that our relationship was doomed because of that. It was too heavy for me. So we broke up. I've never forgiven myself for being so weak and for not standing up for myself.

Cal

We put our needs last, losing ourselves

Don't be afraid of losing people. Be afraid of losing yourself by trying to please everyone around you.

Anonymous

Being a considerate person who cares about others is a good thing.

Difficulties arise when things get out of balance, and we care too much about other people and not enough about ourselves. We can end up living our lives through the eyes of others, completely preoccupied with their opinions and feelings towards us.

I want to make people happy with what I do, especially at work. I can't believe how much I've put up with, just so that my bosses were pleased with me.

Lula

And when we put other people's needs too far above our own, caring so much that we have nothing left for ourselves, we end up depleted and shrivelled up, in a heap on the floor. Our boundaries become so bendy and filled with holes that they collapse. And so do we.

I often struggle when I have to combine the needs of others with my own. But because I am programmed to do what I think the other person wants, my own core needs can be sidelined or suppressed. This is a real problem when I have too many competing priorities to attend to. If I haven't established clear boundaries, then I become overwhelmed and my mental health suffers.

Mae

Once we start down this path, allowing everyone else's needs to come before our own, worrying constantly about what other people think of us, our sense of self becomes eroded. We become trapped by fear of disapproval, negativity, and shame and conflict. We retreat and hide ourselves away, dodging difficult situations and conflict. We avoid expressing our needs and speaking up. We don't want to rock the boat.

A conflict would require me to speak up, and I dread that more than anything. So, I try to avoid that by any means, even if it's at the expense of my happiness and desires.

Stuart

Instead of looking inward to see if what we are doing makes us happy, we are looking outside ourselves all the time, to check what other people think of us. We check in to make sure the way we look and sound is acceptable. Will we pass the test?

It's like being in a high-school clique your whole life. Are you wearing the right shoes? Have you got your socks the right way? Is your hair acceptable? Are you talking the right way, with the right words and the right inflections? Do you have the right stickers on your books?

The right pencil case? Do you speak to the right people? At the right times? You want to fit in, after all.

> *The slightest thing people do to me hurts my feelings and I can't express it to them or stand up for myself because of my shyness. I believe that when I am myself, people don't like me. They like the quiet, nice version of me, so that is who I am around people.*
>
> Dora

Our own internal bully

The more we look outside ourselves, the more we lose the sense of who we really are. The more we allow the perceptions and judgements of others to control us, the more we are trapped by our shyness. This is when we start saying yes to stuff we don't want to do – or no to the stuff we do want.

> *When I have a bad bout of shyness, I literally feel that I'm stupid, not worthy of being listened to, and I want to be swallowed up.*
>
> Rashida

Not content with just checking in with the people around us, and making sure they're happy, we shy bods have gone next level! We've created our own inner bully.

We have a voice in our heads telling us we're no good, judging us, scrutinising our every move. You mucked up last time, you'll never be able to do it. You're rubbish. Nobody gives a crap what you have to say. They think you're useless. They're laughing at you. You're a loser.

I think people are staring at me. I feel pathetic. People are judging me. I assume the kind ones feel sorry for me and the mean ones are laughing at me on the inside.

Aria

Our shyness tells us that our opinions don't matter, that we're no good. It crushes us and controls us.

It's constant. And it's excruciating.

Fear, embarrassment, shame, sadness, discomfort. It makes me feel like I am not a proper adult, that I have these child-like qualities that I 'should' have grown out of. It makes me feel like I'm rubbish, that I am a fake and a fraud, that I don't want my life to be like this.

Ana

Given the chance, our shyness will dominate and control us. Shyness silences us, stops us from seeing our friends, from making phone calls and from connecting with people. It stops us from standing up for ourselves, from speaking up and trying new things.

And here's the thing with bullies: over time, they chip away at your self-esteem, they beat you down, and bit by bit, you start to believe their false accusations. You don't have the energy to stand up and fight back, so eventually, you give in, and stop trying.

Feeling judged and criticised constantly puts us into a state of anxiety. With the threat of judgement looming over us, we worry so much about messing up, that we actually start messing up. We worry about saying the wrong thing, so we get tongue-tied and stumble over our words, and we end up feeling awkward and embarrassed. It's easier, in the end, to avoid the situation in the first place and avoid any negative assessment that goes with it, so we stay silent and hang back in the background.

Then, when we don't speak up, we have the perfect evidence – perfect proof that we are, in fact, a big ol' failure. So it's a vicious circle. The less action we take, the more we withdraw, into a world filled with fear, anxiety and avoidance, under the control of our inner bully.

I feel like I'm shrinking, in size, in confidence and in ambition.

Evelyn

Shyness stops us from showing up as ourselves, from growing and shining.

So self-conscious

I am so self-conscious it's embarrassing. *'Dance like nobody's watching.'* Yeah, right. How would I ever dance like nobody is watching? Even if I was locked in a cellar with three security doors blocking the entrance, I think I would need to be completely drunk before I could even contemplate having a carefree boogie.

I don't like being the centre of attention. I find it deeply uncomfortable. The good thing is that as a twin, (and now as a mum), I rarely am the centre of attention, which suits me just fine. As a kid, I didn't even have to do the whole birthday-party thing on my own. It sure made life easier. I liked the fact that I could always hide behind someone if I needed to. And when my son was little, at big family gatherings I could shift all the focus onto him. Look at the baby, isn't he cute! Sneaky.

When I'm at my boxing gym and learning a new technique, the

instructor might tell me that it's a bit like dancing and that I have to be light on my feet. My immediate thoughts are, 'Oh god, I'm going to be rubbish at this. I don't want to try because I worry I'll look like an idiot. Everyone is going to be looking at me.' I feel like I want to do a runner or hide in the loo because I'm so embarrassed, in advance, about the prospect of looking silly.

Rationally, I can see that this is beyond ridiculous. Firstly, I'm not actually terrible at this stuff. Nobody gets things right the first time. Other people are learning too. And nobody is looking at me; they're all just getting on with it, trying not to trip over their own feet.

When we're with people we know and trust, we can relax, but around new people or those we look up to, we often feel awkward and self-conscious. We worry that they're judging us. It feels like we are being watched all the time. This is actually super weird, considering we hate being watched. We hate being in the spotlight, yet we have chosen to shine a spotlight on our own faces all the time. We hate performing, yet we've turned our lives into a performance. And the fact that nobody is really looking at us, because they're busy living their own lives, doesn't matter – because we've created our own harsh judge in our heads.

We wouldn't talk to anyone else in this way, so why are we talking to ourselves like this?

We are sensitive people who spend a lot of time watching and listening and empathising. These are great skills, but we are not making the most of them because we've allowed our obsession with what's going on in our own minds to dominate us. We are stuck in our own heads, focusing on our own feelings and looking at ourselves.

Off the hook

Newsflash. We are not supreme beings with god-like powers. We are not accountable for anyone other than ourselves.

We can't control other people. We can't *make* anyone, other than ourselves, happy. We can't control how other people act, or what they say, or how they feel, or what they think and believe. We can't control how they treat us, or whether they like us.

We can't choose or control our families or who we are related to. Even though sometimes I'm sure we would like to! We don't govern the laws and rules and structures of the society we live in. We can't influence the weather. We can't really prevent natural disasters. Or disease. We can't control time, or how quickly it seems to fly by. We can't control the fact that life is messy and sometimes things seem to go well and sometimes they don't.

We are carrying too much responsibility for things that we can't control. And we blame ourselves when things go wrong, or when they don't work out perfectly.

Let's say you're invited out for dinner with your friends, but it doesn't quite work out the way you thought it would. The taxi doesn't show up. The service at the restaurant is slow. Someone's food order is wrong. Someone else has a headache and is a bit grumpy. One friend is worried about her kid and has to leave early. It's raining and everyone gets soaked on the way home.

You sit there all night feeling uneasy. And responsible. You want everyone to have a good time. And you're worried that they didn't. Which makes you feel tense and stressed. You try to look on the bright side: it's been ages since you were all together. But you feel yourself going into jazz-hands mode, trying to lift the moods of everyone around you. Like you're the boss of their brains.

It's not your responsibility to make everything awesome. Sometimes it's just a shit party.

When you think about it, it is a little self-important. Why do we assume that we are the one in control of everything? Why do we see ourselves as being the masters of the universe? It's not our job to control everything – from the restaurant's processes and quality control, to the weather! Ensuring everyone has a good time is not on you. You can't make everyone else happy.

We are so ready to blame ourselves for bad stuff that happens. We take responsibility for things that can't possibly be our fault. It's no wonder we feel powerless and overwhelmed! But what about the good stuff? We never take credit for that, do we? No, of course we don't. When someone praises us, or congratulates us, or compliments us, we shrug it off. But we can't have it both ways. We can't live our lives taking responsibility for all the bad stuff and none of the good stuff.

Let's start off letting go of some of that weight. Put it down. Walk away.

The only reactions we can control are our own.

Imagine you see someone in the street who you recognise from school. You make an effort to make eye contact with them and smile, but they blank you completely. How rude! Their ignoring you triggers a reaction in your body. You blush. You shrink down. Shoulders hunched. You feel ashamed. Embarrassed. You start thinking. And this is where your brain starts farting big time. You imagine that this person from school hates you. They deliberately blanked you. Because you're totally uncool. They don't want to be seen with you. You look so old and wrinkly, they didn't recognise you. And you have terrible shoes. All these awful negative thoughts are in your head.

Instead of worrying about what people are thinking, focus instead on what actually happened.

The reality is that this person from school was having a super-stressful day. Their hamster died. Their kid was upset. They had a row with their partner. They were late. The car wouldn't start, so they ran to work. And they were not wearing the right outfit for running, not in any way. They were so caught up in their own world that everything was a blur around them. People, shops, paving slabs. They were so caught up in themselves that a few moments after you saw them, they narrowly missed getting flattened by a truck.

You can choose to see evil and negativity everywhere, or you can decide that people are pretty simple, and most of the time the things they do, and the words that they say are straightforward.

You can't control other people!

By choosing not to look outside yourself for explanations and focusing instead on possible outcomes based entirely on your own sense of self, you are blinded to the truth. Like this person was blinded to the truth.

So, what's next for you? Are you going to walk around like a zombie, with resting bitch face, never smiling at anyone again, just in case they blank you?

If you choose this path, you'll miss out. And all because you imagined that someone blanked you. You can choose how *you* react. But you can't control how someone else reacts.

Their happiness is not my problem

You can't be afraid of what people are going to say, because you're never going to make everyone happy.

Selena Gomez, singer*

We are so worried about messing up, upsetting people or being negatively judged that we live like we are holding the happiness of everyone around us in our hands. And believe me, when you live your life like that, things can get pretty tense.

You can't *make* other people happy. You can only make yourself happy.

I have to tell you that it took me a long time to come to terms with this idea. I thought, Of course I can make other people happy! I can run around after them, doing lots of things for them, not telling them when I'm upset or sad, or annoyed or irritated.

We are *only* responsible for the way *we* feel. We are responsible for our own happiness. You can't run yourself ragged trying to cheer people up all the time. Like some kind of deranged clown.

You can, of course, be a decent human and do your best to be kind to people. You can do nice things, and be full of joy and cheer. But you can't force someone to feel a certain way.

You can make someone a pizza – even a really good pizza – but you can't make them like it. You can dance around in a sexy outfit, but you can't make someone feel things they don't feel. You can tell someone to smile, but they don't necessarily feel happy.

---

* https://www.cosmopolitan.com/entertainment/celebs/news/a41462/inspirational-selena-gomez-quotes/

Conversely, we can't expect other people to make us happy. We are the boss of our emotions. We are responsible for our own happiness. It's up to us to make choices and take control of stuff. We can't look to other people to meet all our needs. We can't expect other people to make us happy. Only we can make ourselves happy.

Caring too much

I think we care too much, about too many things. And we care too much about the wrong things. It's like our caring capacity has gone haywire.

We care what people think of us. We care about them liking us. We care about messing up. We care about being wrong, about not being good enough. We care about people disagreeing with us. And about looking silly. Oh yawn, it's a long list.

It's good to be kind, and responsible and caring. Of course it is. But, we're spread too thin, chucking our cares around willy nilly. Instead of caring about the important stuff – like helping people who matter to us, being kind to ourselves, creating impact in our lives or having loads of mad fun – we are frittering our cares away.

When we care so carelessly, we're placing too much pressure on ourselves.

We end up putting our own wants and needs to one side. It's like we have given so much importance to the feelings of others. We're telling ourselves and the world that we don't matter. That we are not important.

Put the grenade down

I remember when I was a kid walking through the gym hall at school. I must have been about ten. I had a face like thunder. One of the ladies who worked in the office walked past me. 'Cheer up, it might never happen,' she said. And instead of smiling, I muttered, in an overly dramatic fashion: 'It already has.' I can't remember what was going on, but to me, it was a catastrophe.

When something little happens, we can imagine it's the worst thing in the world. Sometimes small becomes insurmountable. It can feel like we are walking around holding a grenade and our words could blow the whole thing up at any moment. As if we have so much power that we freeze. Just in case, you know . . . kaboom – in case we upset someone, or we are not good enough or we mess up. Or we look silly. So we do nothing. We sit still in the corner, holding the imaginary grenade.

But we can choose to put the grenade down, pack it away safely in a box. It's not for us.

Free writing

We get stuck inside our heads on a perpetual mental loop. We're less likely to talk things through, because we're shy, and that prevents us from getting feedback and a fresh perspective on our worries. Repeating our thoughts reinforces our ideas and worries, until we become convinced that they're true. But, if we can find a way to voice our feelings and concerns, we can take a step back and start to see things with objectivity, see things another way.

Expressing our emotions through writing is a shy-person-friendly way to process. When you put pen to paper and your feelings flow out of you onto the page, it helps you understand and deal with things. You may realise that your feelings are a bit extreme, process things in a different way, or find peace. The act of writing stops us silently battling with our brain cells.

Be more Marmite

You can only be truly free when you stop trying to please everyone and make everyone like you, all the time.

When you try to please everyone, you risk not doing anything or saying anything at all. When you try to please everyone, you risk pleasing nobody. You become magnolia. And who actually likes magnolia?

Imagine you write an article. You type it out and print copies. You show it to 100 people. Everyone will have a different opinion on it. A different view. But it's the same thing. How is that possible?

People interpret things differently. They have different values. Different experiences. Different agendas. Different emotions. It's all going to affect their reaction. And you can't control any of that stuff.

Trying to make everyone like you and agree with you all of the time is a pointless exercise! You could dedicate your life to pleasing everyone and you never will.

Some people won't like you. And that's OK. We both know you're brilliant, and if they can't see that, it's their loss. Truly.

Not everyone's opinion matters. Be there for the people who really count. The ones who are important to you. And let the rest go.

Some people are dicks

When you're doing something you care about, like starting a business or writing a book or playing in a football match, you may come up against critics. And assholes.

> *One of the school mums came up to me and asked me how my work was going. I told her that since I'd lost my job, I had decided to retrain and become a personal trainer. She looked me up and down and said, 'Oh, you're hilarious! Well, I guess you've always been quite butch, haven't you?' I wanted to kick her, but I didn't. I felt like all my hope had shattered into a million pieces.*
>
> Lianne

Do you worry about what that cow bag thinks of you? Not so much. Because you've got more important things to get on with. You have a choice. Worry about whether your plans are ridiculous or think, screw you and your opinion, Sandra! I'm busy getting on with my life and career, what are you doing?

The reason people have opinions and make snarky comments is that they often don't have anything going on in their own lives. Or they are jealous. Or they have haemorrhoids. And they're taking it out on you.

Care less about people's comments and opinions. Feel sorry for them instead. Haemorrhoids are awful. Or so I've heard.

You know when you watch a talent show – there are thousands of people there, just willing the person juggling knives and fireballs on the stage to succeed. Because he is brave. For having a go. For daring to try. For daring to show up and step into the ring.

You don't wish for them to fall off the high wire and break all the bones in their body, while also igniting into a massive blaze and slicing themselves into a million pieces on live TV. Only a complete psycho would wish that on someone.

And the same goes for you. When you show up and speak up, people want you to succeed. Because you're stepping into the arena.

If you give a talk, the people who already know what you're saying think, 'Yes, that's right. I agree.' And people who've not heard it before think, 'That's new and interesting.'

People want you to succeed. Most of the time.

The ones who don't want you to succeed – they are not your people. They are dicks. But the ones who love you want you to do well – they're the people you are going to focus on.

Care carefully

Embrace your inner honey badger. Not a euphemism.

And if you haven't seen the famous meme about the 'Crazy Nastyass Honey Badger', narrated by the funniest guy ever, Randall, go watch it!

The honey badgers are just crazeee. Honey badgers are fearless. They don't give a shit. So nasty. Chasing things and eating them. A house full of bees. The honey badger doesn't give a shit. The honey badger goes into a bee nest. Gets stung like a thousand times and he doesn't give a shit! A major battle between a king cobra and a honey badger. Honey badger smacks the shit out of it.

I like the fact that the honey badger doesn't seem to care about anything. He's not held back by fear or worry or wanting to make sure everyone and everything around him is happy. He's just going for it, full throttle.

Being 100 per cent honey badger would probably land us in prison. But what if we were a smidge honey badger? And we cared a touch more carefully?

When you wake up each morning, you have a set amount of energy to spend. You can choose to spend that energy any way you like. You could spend it eating and get more energy – bonus – or you could work out and hone those abs, build something cool, think about things, help others, change the world in some way. Or you could decorate yourself and the space around you, go roller skating, dye your hair purple and have an all-day sex marathon.

Spend your energy wisely.

Don't waste it on stuff that doesn't mean a thing and doesn't make you happy.

Care less about what people think.

Care less about being liked by everyone.

Care less about trying to make everyone happy.

Care less about making a mess and messing up.

Care less about criticism.

Care less about people who don't matter to you.

Care only about the things you really care about.

Care about the big things.

Care about the best people.

Care carefully.

And only then can you become Mighty Free.

MIGHTY MISSION

Try this and become instantly more mighty!

- Make a list of people and things that you really care about. Whose opinions really matter to you?
- Now, go back and look at your list. You only have space for five people or things.
- Who (or what) can you chop?

CHAPTER 13

MIGHTY SNUG

I used to not even be able to order pizza on the phone because I was just so shy. I think that's why so much comes out on-screen, because that's my time to let go in a safe place.

Evan Rachel Wood, actor*

We'd been looking forward to it for months. And when the day finally came, the enormity of the responsibility placed on our shoulders slowly dawned upon us. It was our son's turn to take the nursery-school teddy bear home for the weekend.

This assignment was sacred. A once-in-a-lifetime opportunity. It was up to us as a family to take care of the bear – feed him, entertain him, take him on adventures and ensure he made it back in one piece the following week. Every detail of these shenanigans was to be documented in a special notebook, ready to be shared with the class.

I pored over the notebook, swotting up on the bear's past adventures, all written up meticulously by parents who clearly had nothing better to do than make out their three-year-old was a literary genius.

---

* https://m.imdb.com/name/nm0939697/quotes

I took our bear care duties very seriously indeed. I lived in fear that we would be the ones who damaged or lost our special guest.

We let the bear watch his favourite TV shows, we dressed him, pampered him, invited him to dinner, involved him in scintillating discussions and took him on outings. We were kind to him. We provided the bear necessities – and more. For that unforgettable weekend, he was one of the family.

We took care of a stinky, matted, old teddy bear, who was undoubtedly coated in generations of snot. We were kind to a piece of mangy old fur. And actually, it wasn't that hard.

So, if being kind to something so gross is easy, then why can't we be kind to ourselves?

Shy people have a mean streak

We're compassionate and kind-hearted towards others. We are empathetic and sympathetic. We care. But not about ourselves.

And it's not just that we are 'not that kind' to ourselves. We haven't got a little lax on the ol' self-care. It goes beyond that. We are super mean to ourselves. We treat ourselves worse than we would treat any other person, animal or minging old lump of stuffing.

As if being shy wasn't hard enough, we've decided to take it up a notch, deferring to the inner bully we met earlier. Our inner bully has taken over. Let's call him Dick. We've all got a Dick inside us. He's horrible. He's controlling and abusive. And he needs to stand down.

The fact that we sometimes struggle to speak up means that so many of our thoughts are internalised. We talk to Dick a lot. He likes nothing more than to squash us and to silence us. And when we fall short of our very high expectations, our inner Dick is there, ready to tell us smugly how he knew we would fail.

We hate confrontation, and yet we're constantly confronting ourselves. Oh, the irony. Poking, dismissing, berating, damning. We are harsh and mean, constantly criticising ourselves, telling ourselves we are worthless and that we don't matter.

We would never talk to another person the way we talk to ourselves.

All people, shy or outgoing, deserve good things. We deserve love. We deserve kindness. We deserve respect.

We deserve to get those things from other people, and from ourselves.

A kinder voice

Looking back, I would say that shyness has held me back. It affected many aspects of my life, from friendships to work. But so much of it was about my relationship with myself. I often feel I need to work harder on being my own best friend, to speak up for myself and stay positive.

Liz

According to *The Brain* (a PBS documentary series created and presented by neuroscientist Dr David Eagleman), we say between 300 to 1,000 words to ourselves every minute! So, let's make those words positive ones.

US Navy SEALs have embraced positive self-talk. When they are deep underwater, deprived of oxygen and dealing with stressful situations, they use positive words to help themselves handle everything that is thrown at them.

Imagine you're talking to a cute, furry, wriggly puppy. Ahhh. He accidentally pees on the carpet. Oopsie.

What would you do?

Bend down and say in a soft voice: 'That's ok. Try peeing outside next time. Let's get this cleaned up, shall we little fluff?'

Stand over him in a menacing manner and shout, 'You are a piece of crap! You messed up. I hate you. You're useless.'

I think we can safely assume that you'd go with option A.

Next question.

Your friend missed out on an opportunity at work. They were too scared to put themselves forward and they are disappointed in themselves.

How would you react?

A) Reassure them that it's ok. Listen to them. Validate their feelings. Tell them you're proud of them and help them to figure out how to go after the next opportunity.

B) Grab them by the shoulders and shout in their face, 'You're a complete failure! You deserve nothing. You're a total loser. I hate you.'

I'm assuming you're not a total asshole, and you went with option A.

We listen to our friends, we offer advice and we encourage them. We might ask them questions and seek to understand what's really going on. We help them to process their feelings and look for solutions. We don't dismiss their struggles and dramas. We don't tell them to shut up and get a grip.

And yet.

We don't extend this kindness and compassion to ourselves.

It's time we started, don't you think? From now on, let's start talking to ourselves like we are a good friend. Or a cute, fuzzy puppy.

Cheesy? A little. But it's worth a shot.

Ask yourself:

How would my best friend talk to me right now?

What advice would they give me?

How would they encourage me or reassure me?

Being compassionate to ourselves makes us feel good. We release more of the hormone oxytocin, which helps us feel calm and safe — it's the warm fuzzies. And this feeling helps us to take action, to do the things we need to do.

The journey to becoming more mighty is long. We all know that road trips are more fun when you're with a friend. So, let's start by being a decent kind of friend to ourselves.

And next time your inner Dick pipes up, check yourself. Would you say it to a friend? If not, tell Dick to shut his hole.

Adrenaline dumping

Being shy can be stressful.

Everyday situations, like ordering a coffee, bumping into an acquaintance at the bus stop, or raising an issue with a colleague, causes us to feel awkward, stressed and self-conscious. Our bodies shake, our hearts pump like a piston, we blush and we sweat. Feeling uncomfortable and exposed raises our levels of anxiety.

And when we're stressed, we release two hormones: cortisol and adrenaline. Adrenaline (or epinephrine in America — now all those episodes of *Grey's Anatomy* make sense) gives your heart a jolt and makes it beat like a drum; it boosts your energy, so you're ready for battle. Adrenaline is a quick hit, but cortisol is a long-term fix. It increases the levels of glucose in your blood and helps your brain to become more alert. It also suppresses areas that aren't needed here, like your reproductive organs and your digestion.

Adrenaline is designed to give us superhero strength, in dangerous moments, just for a short time so that we can save the day. But once the surge is over, we're left with an adrenaline dump. The danger has gone, so your adrenaline and cortisol levels fall. This sudden drop causes a bunch of unfortunate side effects, from puking, or crying, to uncontrollable giggles or even peeing. Oh, and all that adrenaline uses up a load of oxygen and energy, leaving you feeling knackered and in need of a nap. Once the pressure is off, we're hard pressed to function at all. We crash and burn.

What if your shyness makes you feel anxious, a lot of the time? Your fight-or-flight response is always on, your stress response system is activated, and stress hormones, particularly cortisol, continue to pump around your body. And if you've always got cortisol flooding your body, it can lead to stomach issues, heart disease, weight gain, headaches and sleep strife. Lots of not great things.

We're riding the anxiety rollercoaster every single day. It's no wonder we feel wrung out. Like top athletes, we have to take special care of ourselves, to manage our energy and the pressure we place upon ourselves, so that we can unleash our shy potential when it really counts.

We need comfort, kindness and safety to function and to thrive. We need snugness to shine.

Confined to comfort

Comfort zones get a bad press. The internet is littered with articles and memes telling us how staying in our comfort zone is boring, it's the enemy of personal growth, it's lazy and dull and leads to us languishing in our own filth, wearing sweatpants covered in suspect stains, not having showered in days.

Successful people tell us we should hustle hard. Management gurus believe that anxiety boosts performance, that adrenaline fuels success. Rarrr! According to influencers and gurus all over Instagram, chilling out in our comfort zone is a sign that we're stagnating in the swamp of underachievement.

But I believe we're getting mugged off by all these inspirational mugs (and I'm not calling the people mugs; I'm talking about actual mugs you drink tea out of), proclaiming that comfort zones kill dreams and success.

Why would I choose to live my life feeling uncomfortable? That sounds like a terrible idea. Shudder.

We shy people know what it's like to feel anxious. It doesn't help us to perform or achieve our best. It's no way to live. It's not good for us. It can make us ill. We need to feel comfortable, so that we can push ourselves forwards sometimes. We need a safe space to come back to when we're done pushing; space and time to recuperate, recover and regain the strength we need to press on again.

If we push and push and press and press, constantly confronting our fears with no rest, we flood our bodies with cortisol. We live in a constant state of anxiety, manically veering from one shyness crisis to the next.

But if we feel comfortable and safe and snug, living in our comfort zone, or ever so slightly beyond it, we have the strength and security we need to take little steps, building a life and a future for ourselves, one day at a time.

I have favourite sweaters. They are cosy and comfortable and I feel like myself. I wear these instead of dressing up when I go to events where I need to be social. This helps me feel safe in a situation where I usually don't. Once I went to a big networking party directly from a workout class, in my workout clothes, totally sweaty. I looked like shit. And it was the best! I had major post-exercise endorphins, I wasn't trying to be cute, no lipstick or dressing up which makes me feel fake. I didn't feel like I was pretending and failing, I was 100 per cent being myself, and it made me feel confident.

Ruth

Safety first

When we don't feel safe, it's hard to focus on anything else. Your body and brain are preoccupied with trying to make sure you're not about to plunge to your death.

When we are physically safe, we know we are not going to get eaten by a monster, because we have a house with windows and doors, which means we can relax, watch telly and eat our dinner in peace. Living far enough away from volcanoes, fault lines and cliff edges increases the likelihood that our houses will not implode, explode or fall off a sharp ravine in the near future. We've handed in our machetes and guns, there are no live wires hanging from the walls, we've had the gas checked, there are no poisonous substances lying around and the dog doesn't seem to have rabies.

Knowing that we are not at imminent risk of injury, violence or threat is pretty nice. It's a primal and basic need.

There's another kind of safety, though. Psychological or emotional safety. It's not something we can see; there are no skull and crossbones stickers to alert us to danger. But emotional danger, or social threat, arises when we are met with mockery, ridicule, rage, blame, bullying or rudeness.

Emotional safety is important. It's something we need to think about more. It can have a huge impact on our lives. It's important in the home, at school, in relationships, in teams, in sport and in the workplace. When people feel safe, they feel able to speak up.

And it's particularly important for us shy people.

Family, friends, my lifelong teddy, my cat – all of them giving me simple cuddles! My teddy bear, Jackie, used to make me feel safe as a child, and my big brother, who was like a superhero to me.

Juno

We feel emotionally safe when we trust the people around us, when we feel like we can take risks without being judged or criticised. We feel comfy being ourselves.

In situations where people respect each other, they feel like they can ask for help, own up to mistakes, admit they messed up, talk openly about things that have gone wrong. People feel free to try new things, to experiment and take risks.

When we believe that we are psychologically safe, we feel able to try new things and push ourselves forward. When we feel safe, we are able to be creative, to share our work and ideas and our deepest feelings and thoughts, to express our true selves, to be vulnerable and honest, and to speak freely.

We deserve to feel safe in all areas of our lives, so that we can blossom and flourish. We deserve to feel safe and comfortable in our homes, friendships, relationships, schools, social circles and work-places.

Surround yourself with people who nurture and nourish you. People who understand and support you. The ones you could call in the middle of the night if there was a massive spider. These are the people you need in your life.

> *I feel safe with my boyfriend and my best friend. I feel safe alone. I need people who understand me, who like me for me and don't see my shyness as a bad thing.*
>
> Roxy

Choose workplaces that welcome open dialogue and feedback, different personalities and viewpoints. Choose the ones that embrace learning and mistakes. Choose workplaces that bring out the best in you. Work is not prison. If you don't like it, you don't have to stay.

Spend time with people who encourage you to speak up, ask questions and share your opinions. People who encourage you to be yourself.

> *I used to have a friend who would constantly shame me. He would say things like, 'You always do stupid things', 'You're too quiet', 'You're so moody'. I found his words harsh. He made me feel bad about myself. It took me a long time to realise that I don't deserve to be spoken to like that.*
>
> Lyn

Box clever

People don't like the fact that I love boxing. They find it weird. However, some people, including my grandmas, surprisingly, think it's cool. They encourage and support me. But others, often those I would expect to back me, don't. I feel like they're trying to change me. They don't like me going to the gym or hanging out with my gym friends.

They make funny comments about it. I feel like they're judging me and talking about me behind my back. In fact, I know they are. It really doesn't make me want to spend time with them.

When we feel like we're not being emotionally supported, that's when we clam up, close the door and keep our feelings to ourselves. When we're worried about being criticised, or rejected or ignored or talked over, we learn that keeping quiet is the best option.

I was trying to tell her about my work, that it was really hard and that I was struggling. But every time I tried to talk about it, she changed the subject, or talked over me. In the end I stopped talking about it and just withdrew even further.

Nick

When we feel safe, we can show up as we are. We can be ourselves, not constantly criticised or berated for not being how someone wants us to be. It's not asking a lot, to be surrounded by people who are kind and considerate.

Safety is not boring. Comfortable is not humdrum. When we feel safe, we can talk about our feelings, and our wants and needs and our worries. We don't get defensive and angry and nitpicky. When we feel safe, we are free to be creative, to love, to laugh and to really live our lives. When we feel safe, we are free to become more mighty.

A stressed brain cannot think straight

Our brain is programmed to be alert to danger. It uses a system called neuroception, to process feelings in our bodies, and figure out if people or situations are dangerous and then put the correct action into place.

If we assess that an incoming hug is safe, we can relax and connect with the other person. If we view a hug from a stranger as creepy, we freeze up, or take evasive action.

When we feel safe, both physically and emotionally, the social-engagement part of our brains chills out too. We can start thinking more clearly. We can be creative, listen, empathise, collaborate, chat to other people and enjoy a cuddle.

When we feel unsafe, all our brain power and physical resources move into protection mode. And it's not just that we won't want to talk openly or experiment or try new things. It's physically more challenging to learn new things or to focus on being brave if we feel unsafe. When we feel anxious, insecure, embarrassed, awkward or afraid our brains are in panic mode, focusing on the lion, rather than concentrating on being more mighty. We need to feel calm, comfy, safe and snuggly in order to take in information, concentrate, make good decisions, take risks and achieve our goals.

This goes way beyond pampering and self-care. It's science!

Pushing ourselves forward places demands on our brains. And, just like the brains of a professional athlete, for our brains to perform at a higher level they need the right kind of conditions.

When we feel stressed out, our brain turns to mush. Well, kind of. The front of our brain is called the prefrontal cortex (PFC). It controls deep thinking, our ability to plan or have ideas, and regulate our emotions. Important stuff. When we are stressed, this advanced part of the brain goes offline. You don't want to be thinking deep thoughts, pondering the meaning of life or coming up with the plot for your next novel when you're about to fight a lion. In times of stress and danger, our brains need to be able to fight or flee.

When we are stressed out for long periods of time, perhaps because home, work or relationships are not safe and supportive, we stay in the primitive part of our brain, ready to leap into fight mode. Prolonged stress can even lead to us losing connections between the prefrontal cortex and the other areas of the brain.

So, that's why when you feel intimidated or judged or constantly poked at and criticised, you start stumbling over your words, you feel overly emotional, you can't remember key things and find it harder to form coherent sentences. When you're stressed, the thinking part of your brain is offline.

It's hard to be mighty when you can't string a sentence together.

Emotional safety is like a net underneath us, ready to catch us if we fall. And because we know it's there, we feel able to take a risk, to step out onto the tightrope – because if we fall off, we are not going to end up splattered all over the floor.

The only reason I am able to get into a boxing ring is because I have turned the comfort blanket that I was hiding underneath into a safety net. Knowing there is a fuzzy, bouncy blanket underneath me, ready to catch me if I need it, makes me feel physically and emotionally safe.

I have the right coach, the right training programme, the right nutrition plan, the right shoes, the right gloves, the right gumshield and, most importantly, the right shiny shorts.

It's all in place. Creating comfort and safety around me and knowing that I am being looked after gives me the feeling of security and strength.

There's a world of possibility, growth and opportunity out there, just waiting for us. But to get there we need to feel safe and secure enough, physically and emotionally, to step out of the shadows and into a bigger life.

We just need to know our safety net is in place.

Feeling swaddled

Aside from controlling the situations we find ourselves in, and the people we're around, how else can we create a feeling of safety and snugness for ourselves?

Well, we can make ourselves feel snug and safe in lots of different ways – from the clothes we wear, to the TV shows we watch and the way we design our homes. The possibilities for snugness are everywhere.

We can start by creating the feeling that we are being enveloped in a big warm hug. Ahhh. I'm a big fan of fuzzy fashion: cashmere lounge-wear, a warm scarf, fleece hoodies, fluffy socks, a super-soft onesie and Ugg boots. Bliss. I am also rather partial to big knickers and high-waisted trousers. How very all-encompassing. (Although I'm not sure channelling the rather rotund Obelix of Asterix fame is a good look!)

When I'm giving a talk or doing something scary, I like to wear dungarees. I think having a thick piece of denim on my body and some solid straps makes me feel protected. It's like armour. And I personally think they look kinda cute – as long as I don't turn sideways, in which case, I look eight months pregnant.

The fact that wearing comfies makes me feel safe and relaxed isn't random. According to research, wearing soft textures or compression-style clothes may help us to feel calmer. Pressure on the body helps the brain to release the happy, snuggly chemical serotonin.

I feel safe and snug when I wear my favourite woolly scarf. I wear it all the time! My craft room makes me feel safe too. I have lots of fairy lights in there, and I like to light scented candles too, to create a really cosy atmosphere.

Sam

Designing a cosy retreat in your home gives you somewhere to relax and recuperate after a tough day of being mighty. Somewhere toasty with comforting blankets, scented candles, relaxing music and peace and quiet will soothe your soul and help you recover from your exertions.

I feel safest at home. I think calming scents like lavender really help, also a warm bath and candlelight, so a lot of sensory things. It helps to remove me from the outside world. I think living in a city is quite bad for my mental health, so it helps to feel like you can retreat within your home and find peace and quiet there.

Tilly

Hug the dog

When I'm ill, sad or stressed, Bobby the dog comes to my rescue. It's like he knows I need a hug and it's his job to help me. Scientists have proven that snuggling a furry pet has a soothing effect on us.

There are a few things in my life that make me feel safe; my dad and my step-mum always make me feel safe because they're really nice to me and understand me. And this might sound weird, but my pet rabbit makes me feel safe. I don't really know why – I just feel like she's there for me.

Priya

Petting our pets makes us feel good. It's why therapy dogs or horses go into schools, hospitals, nursing homes, hospices and even courtrooms, to help people heal and feel less anxious. When we stroke a pet, or gaze lovingly into their eyes, the hormone oxytocin is released, helping us to relax and feel a lot less stressed.

Bobs, where are you? I need a snuggle.

Comfort eating

Comfort food is good for you. No, really. We all know that chicken soup is good for the soul. And I would argue that a bowl of macaroni cheese has equal healing powers.

Comfort food works because it reminds us of when we were kids. It's taking a step back in time, back to the safety and security of childhood, with those fond memories of being taken care of.

There are times when indulging in a pint of ice cream or a gallon of mash will make us feel good. But there are other types of food that can help us to feel less anxious and won't lead to lardiness.

I don't want this to sound like a big ol' lecture about being healthy, because I know just how boring and annoying that is. But what if I told you that the food we stuff in our faces could be making us feel more anxious?

If we're stressed and anxious a lot of the time, then our cortisol stays elevated and we end up storing fat, and not in the good places. Too much cortisol can make us ill too. It increases inflammation and suppresses our immune systems. And that can lead to colds and flu but also increase our risk of allergies, stomach problems, auto-immune diseases and even cancer.

Too much caffeine can also make us feel stressed and buzzy and it can raise our cortisol levels. I mean, we've all had the jitters, or felt the crash, right? I'm not going to give up caffeine altogether, or I'll be a total bitch in the mornings, but limiting caffeine intake to one or two cups of coffee a day, or perhaps having sugar-free, caffeine-free, fun-free Diet Coke is a start. Try camomile tea, a turmeric latte or a fruit tea instead.

Clearly, filling your face with sugar is also gonna be a bad idea. I'm not going to harp on too much about this because I do have a major sweet tooth. It's not all bad news for chocoholics though, because, apparently, eating a small amount of dark chocolate can help reduce stress and anxiety. I'm not a big fan, but it's better than nothing, I guess.

Aside from avoiding stimulants, we could also try making healthier choices and eating more veggies, fruit, beans, grains, pulses and protein, which can help to reduce inflammation. Fatty fish containing omega-3 can help reduce inflammation too. Fermented foods like yoghurt are good for your gut bacteria and have been linked to reducing anxiety.

For a quick snack, brazil nuts contain selenium, which can reduce inflammation and give you a mood boost.

A big ol' daily dose of vitamin D has been suggested to improve your immune function and it has also been said that it can help boost your mood and reduce levels of anxiety. Which makes sense, considering being in the sunshine does that too. Eggs contain vitamin D, and they are a good source of protein. They also contain tryptophan, an amino acid that helps create serotonin, a chemical neurotransmitter which can help to boost our brain function and relieve anxiety.

Other snacks like pumpkin seeds and bananas which contain lots of potassium can help boost our mood too. Pumpkin pie. Banana and brazil nut cake. As if we needed an excuse?

Mighty moves

A few years ago, I committed to exercising most days.

I had spent a few years getting into some pretty destructive habits, such as pigging out on crap and then feeling really bad about myself. And because I got fat and spotty, I didn't look how I wanted to look, which gave me another reason to hide away.

I had all kinds of excuses going on. And I really couldn't be arsed to exercise much. Nor could I be arsed to stop eating rubbish.

And then, by accident, I found something I actually liked. I had the opportunity to put on some boxing gloves and hit a punch bag. And it changed my life.

I fell in love with boxing. And the sound of the smash. It's so exhilarating and sweaty. And I've never had so much fun. Now, I feel like I can't live without it. It's become a non-negotiable. It makes me feel so good. So, I find the time to train most days. Even when I'm busy or tired or whatever.

Previously, I never thought I had the time. I felt like prioritising myself was selfish or that I didn't deserve to have fun. But, I do deserve it. And when I feel good and strong and relaxed and calm, I'm also a lot nicer to be around. Plus, I love that I get to release all my pent-up stress and frustration and, occasionally, a little bit of rage. No matter what's happened that day, I feel so much better after I've trained.

Exercise is good for our bodies and our brains. Moving our muscles, even for just a few minutes a day helps to reduce stress. It reduces tension, boosts our mood, helps us sleep better. And we all know that when we feel good in our bodies, it makes us feel better in ourselves.

Exercise releases endorphins and other good chemicals that make us feel good. When we're busy trying to hit a ball or a punch bag, we're not thinking about our worries or the fact that we're shy. Achieving things makes us feel good. Lifting those weights or running as fast as our legs will carry us gives us a sense of achievement. And knowing that your muscles are poppin' will make you feel pretty fly.

Plus, exercise is fun. And it's a good way to meet people and make new friends without too much effort. People just seem to chat to each other when they're working out or doing a sport. It's easy and natural. Before you know it, you'll be hanging out with your gym fam.

Mighty mindful

Meditation and breathing techniques or yoga are a great way to calm your mind and your body. Even just breathing in and out slowly. Pausing. And resting for a few minutes. We spend our lives rushing, rushing around. I don't know about you, but sometimes I feel like I'm living in a constant state of stress, racing about, remembering all the things I have to do. Rush, rush, rush. It's ridiculous. When I feel like this, I'll plop down on the sofa for a moment and try to breathe, in and out, slowly. And regroup.

And if I'm about to go and do something scary, I'll breathe in and out deeply. Trying to send my breath to the ends of my fingers, down into my body and into my toes.

I love that nobody can see me doing it.

The day of my first fight, I nearly keeled over with anxiety. I arrived at the venue and saw the ring. The adrenaline was pumping through me. My fingers and arms felt all tingly and funny. I looked as white as a sheet. After the medical check-up, there was a long wait. I was freaking out.

I went and sat down in a quiet corner, with my headphones on, listening to calming music. I tried to read a trashy novel, with a rather incongruous title – *A Spring Affair*, or something about a tea shop. And tried to slow my breathing from a dog-like pant to a calm yogi-style breath.

To relieve nerves and stress, try breathing in through your nose for four, five seconds. And then slowly exhale, for five or even six seconds. Focus just on your body and relaxing each part of you. Keeping it calm, and consistent.

Rest up

There's a reason why a boxing match is divided into rounds. Nobody could fight for a solid half hour without keeling over. And if they did try, they'd be pretty rubbish! Instead, you push hard for three minutes and have a rest for sixty seconds. During the break, you get to have a nice sit-down, regulate your breathing, have a sip of water, a little chat with your coach and get patched up with some weird goo. And then you go again.

Life is like that. Push hard. Rest. Go again.

Embracing new challenges and facing our fears uses up a lot of energy. It's hard to be mighty if you've worked yourself into a state of exhaustion. You can't push yourself forward and smash your way through life constantly. You'll burn out.

Athletes understand that rest days actually help you to achieve your goals more quickly. Taking a break from working out gives muscles time to heal, recuperate and grow stronger. It also enables the nervous system to regenerate. Resting discourages us from overtraining, which can lead to injury or burn out.

Whether you choose to spend ten hours or ten minutes relaxing, make them count. Snuggle up on the sofa with a cuppa, walk barefoot on the grass, take a long soak in a bubbly bath, walk the dog somewhere breath-taking, dance to your favourite album of all time, luxuriate for hours at a spa, get your yogi on, stitch and bitch with friends. Any or all of the above. But probably not at the same time.

> *I feel safe when I'm listening to music. I like going into my study room and blasting music the most. (Dancing may or may not be involved.)*
>
> Tara

And if you're not good at remembering to relax, why not instigate a Mighty Morning routine. Once the chaos has calmed, and I've stopped rushing around like a lunatic, shouting at people and scrabbling around to find a lone shin-pad sleeve (don't ask), I like to sit down for a few beautiful minutes with a cup of coffee and a notebook and plan my day. I realise it's not exactly a spa experience, but I like planning. It stops me feeling scattered. I feel like I'm in control of my life. Maybe I make a list or two. Oooh, now you're talking.

> *Reading a book that 'speaks' to me helps me relax. Cleaning my fridge does too. Knowing my house is clean feels good. My home makes me feel safe, my family make me feel safe.*
>
> Elliot

Putting your needs first, even for just a few minutes, is good for everyone around you.

Mighty sleep

The ultimate form of relaxation? Sleep.

Sleep is a joy. And it's a simple way to take care of body and mind. When we feel anxious our bodies use energy. And being shy makes us feel anxious a lot. Our bodies need sleep to regenerate and recover, particularly after we've pushed ourselves to do something scary.

There's a reason it's called beauty sleep. In the interests of science, Jennifer Lopez gets a solid eight hours a day, because she believes that having a strong sleep game is nature's most powerful beauty secret. It seems to be working well for her.

I love to sleep. I'm a strong power napper. Before a big talk, for example, I often have a little snooze. There's no greater form of relaxation, after all – perhaps apart from being unconscious or in a coma. After a big event, once the adrenaline has stopped pumping around my body, sleep is the perfect way to recover.

Sleep is not weakness. Sleep is kindness.

I can't bear it when people boast about how little sleep they get by on, like it's a contest. It's not a competition to see who can sleep the least – or the most. Be sensible. Listen to your body, and not necessarily to a tracking device. Personally, I can't think of anything less conducive to sleep than knowing my sleep statistics, but that might just be me. Knowing my numbers don't look good is not going to help me relax. It's going to stress me out even more.

Sleeping well is important to keep us healthy and feeling good in our body and our brain. It's even been shown to help us live longer. When we sleep, our cells and muscles and neurones regenerate. Without sleep, apparently we start to malfunction.

And because we often feel anxious, getting sleep is particularly important for us shy people. The irony is, however, that although we might need sleep, grabbing hold of it when we're feeling anxious is like trying to grab a slippery eel. Oh, and sleep deprivation makes us feel more anxious and less able to deal with anxiety when we have it. Bloody marvellous. Talk about a triple whammy.

Love your bed. I do. It's my safe place. I relax and recover in bed. I snuggle. I read. I write. (I'm writing this in my bed, with the dog on my toes.) Obviously, I do other things in my bed, but that's a conversation for another day, and you probably don't need to hear all the details.

For many years, throughout childhood and my teens, I loved my pillow and would seek solace in it. Literally, bury my head in its soft, familiar smell. My bed is my sanctuary from the world.

Barbara

Make sure your bed is a comfy, delicious place to be. Choose the finest linen you can afford, the most feathery, squishy pillows and a supportive mattress. Clear your bedroom of clutter and noise and lights (and people who snore loudly!).

If you struggle to sleep well, try to train yourself to get into a rhythm by going to bed and waking up at the same time, even on weekends. Avoid drinking five pints of lager or four cups of coffee before bed – actually, after lunch, if we're being really sensible. Although, who drinks lager in the morning?

Setting a sleep routine, and going to bed and waking at the same time each day, will help your body get into a good habit. As I said, I love a 20-minute power nap, but post-2pm, it leads to a totally messed-up, sleepless night. As does a three-hour power nap, it turns out.

Calm your mind and your body with yoga or meditation. Embrace sleep rituals, like having a bath, using a calming massage oil or reading a book before bed to help you wind down.

Skip the screens before bed; the blue light keeps you awake. And stop doomscrolling – reading about natural disasters, death, destruction and the end of the world leads to extremely unblissful dreams.

If you struggle to get to sleep (like me), listen to a podcast or some really calming music to help you doze off. Choose earphones that won't strangle you or squish your ears. Or read a very boring book. Not this one, obviously!

If you can't sleep, don't toss and turn for hours. Get up and have a change of scene – maybe go into a different room, read a little and then try again.

If light or noise (from the aforementioned snorer) disturb you, use a silk eye mask, earplugs or headphones. If not, a pillow over their face should do it!

There are no prizes for being the most bedraggled, exhausted, burnt-out person – a withered husk of a human. Pushing ourselves to be more mighty can feel uncomfortable at times. And being shy makes life hard enough, so let's take good care of ourselves, shall we?

MIGHTY MISSION

Try this and become instantly more mighty!

Creating a snuggly safety net supports us and gives us the freedom we need to become more mighty:

- Design your safety net.
- How will you bring a bit more snuggliness and safety into your life?
- Will you watch some comfort TV, order a fleecy onesie, make your bed even more snuggly, or think about ways you could create psychological safety at work?

CHAPTER 14

MIGHTY FIGHT

Let's go Champ. Let's go Champ. Let's go Champ.
Shannon 'The Cannon' Briggs, heavyweight boxer

The Story of Thug Rose

As they stood eyeball to eyeball, the fearsome UFC fighter Joanna Jędrzejczyk unleashed an angry stream of insults at her opponent. Joanna's psychological warfare ripped into her rival's difficult childhood, her mental state, her family, her skills and prowess. Her goal was clear. She intended to unpick her, belittle her, mess with her mind. To hit her where it hurt.

The underdog, Rose Namajunas, aka Thug Rose, did not react to the torrent of abuse. She did not allow herself to feel. She maintained eye contact while Joanna was shouting directly in her face, and still she did not flinch or move a muscle. She knew that no matter what was said, this woman would not have any impact on her mindset.

Then, barely perceptibly, Rose began mumbling to herself, over and over. 'Confidence. Conditioning. Composure. Content. I am a Champion.' Her mantra. She spoke softly, almost silently. These words, repeated rhythmically, were not meant for the public or for her adversary. These mighty words helped Rose to focus, to go within herself and find strength, calm and courage. No aggression, hype, insults, drama or intimidation could wound or unsettle her. She had found a way, without fuss or noise, to tap into her inner strength. As she repeated her mantra, Rose was almost in a hypnotic trance, bringing a sense of calm and peace to her mind, even in the face of a very angry woman.

More than just having a calming effect, mantras train our unconscious minds to believe the words we are saying, to such an extent that they impact our actual conscious behaviour. By repeating her mantra over and over, Rose became the epitome of 'Confidence. Conditioning. Composure. Content.' And she became a champion.

Rose went on to smash Joanna Jędrzejczyk, showing that you really do have to watch the quiet ones.

After the fight she said, 'It's just me that I'm fighting against. Your mind is just another muscle that you can train and get stronger.'

Rose Namajunas is not the only fighter to tap into the power of a mantra. After he lost to Vitali Klitschko in 2010, heavyweight boxer Shannon 'The Cannon' Briggs fell into a deep depression. So he developed a mantra that would inspire and energise him to get back to fitness and get his head back in the ring.

He would chant 'Let's go Champ. Let's go Champ. Let's go Champ' over and over to himself.

And you know what. It worked.

Mighty inside

I don't think of myself as a particularly strong person. I'm not the biggest or the loudest or the bravest. There have been times when I've been barged out the way, sidelined and trodden on. I've melted, surrendered too easily, failed to speak up, followed the crowd and allowed things to happen to me. There have been times when I've felt weak and ashamed and dominated; like my voice was too little or too quiet to be heard.

Usually, I spend far too much time and energy worrying about upsetting or hurting other people. Being aggressive used to feel so alien to me. I was a bit of a wimp, physically and emotionally. If someone was horrible to me, it would affect me for days. I didn't see myself as strong, and I worried that those things were not feminine qualities.

But underneath all my softness, buried rather a long way down – deep, deep down, somewhere between my chest and my tummy and my guts and my brain – I have discovered that I am actually quietly powerful. I'm mighty inside.

We are all made up of a complicated mixture of things. I'm sweet, shy and kind. But I am also feisty, unruly and strong. I believe there's a mighty beast inside all of us. We just have to learn to tap into it.

There's mightiness inside all of us

Being adorable doesn't work in the boxing ring. Go figure.

When I first started boxing, I felt like everyone was laughing at me because they thought I didn't deserve to be there, or because I looked ridiculous. I don't think I've ever felt so self-conscious. I felt like a fish out of water; or an overweight, middle-aged woman in a boxing gym.

I didn't like all the sweat, the smell, the noises or the pain. When training sessions were hard, I gave up too easily. And don't tell anyone, but one time I broke a nail and I honestly felt like crying.

And then there was the punching. It's one thing to punch a heavy bag or the pads, but when someone is punching you back, that's a whole different bloody ballgame. I used to shut my eyes when a punch flew towards my face, and on occasion I have been known to cry 'Eek!' which is not an aspirational boxing technique.

I was an absolute wimp. But I persisted. I adored the way punching stuff made me feel. The impact and the thwack. It was exhilarating. I developed muscles in places I didn't know muscles could be. And as my technique improved, the more motivated I felt, the harder I worked and the better my results got.

Then I had my first fight. And that's when everything really changed.

Prior to that, my main concerns had been how to handle the ring walk without getting the giggles, how to clamber between the ropes without tripping over and falling on my face and whether my bum would look big in my shorts. (Incidentally, I did laugh a little, I didn't fall over and my bum looked huge.)

I had a game plan and some strategies in mind, but they all flew out the window, more or less immediately. We touched gloves. The bell rang and my opponent came at me like a raging beast. In that moment, I realised that I had a choice. I could worry about being mean, or looking silly, or what I was having for dinner and end up getting flattened. Or I could fight back. I chose beast mode.

The fact that I was able to have an actual fight in front of hundreds of people, and not melt under the pressure, makes me realise that there is more mightiness inside me than I ever imagined. And the fact that it's buried deep down means that instead of a veneer, those qualities are part of my core; part of who I am.

With dedication and commitment, we are all capable of big, brave things. We all have mightiness inside us. We just have to choose to go after it.

Shyness is our strength

So, shyness is our thing. It certainly makes life intriguing; don't you think? Shyness makes life challenging; we know that. But what if the shambles of our shyness, our struggle, is what makes us mighty?

We shy people have plenty going on. We face challenges in all kinds of situations – from coffee shops to classrooms, from meetings to meet-ups. Perhaps we face more challenges than outgoing and loud people; or maybe we just face different ones.

Like at the gym. If you want peachy butt cheeks, you can do endless squats or glute bridges. Or you can do squats or glute bridges with an evil resistance band around your thighs. Owww. It's the resistance that makes you stronger.

Pain, mess and grind are useful. They build our strength. Without adversity there is no opportunity to build that strength. We've positioned perfection and gloss as the ideal scenario, when, in fact, we need a bit of spit and grit to help us learn and develop.

Imagine if everything just fell into place for you. All the time. If nothing was tricky or hard. You'd glide along, with success, doughnuts and unicorn sprinkles landing in your lap. You'd never really have to try.

Until you do. Until the day when people are not there to bail you out. Or to give you every little thing your heart desires. Then what? You don't have the skills you need to sort yourself out.

Struggle and challenge are part of life's rich tapestry. And as my dad always used to say, they are character building. Although, when he used to tell us that, we rolled our eyes in such an overly dramatic teenage fashion, we risked permanent injury.

Shyness is our struggle. And it makes us stronger. How do you feel when you finally muster up the courage to speak up in a meeting, or have that difficult conversation, or present your work, or give that talk? Marvellous! You feel like an absolute legend.

The fact that things are not easy makes us appreciate them more. And when we finally do conquer our fears, we speak up and show up with a quiet power that is hard to ignore. We are mighty in spite of our shyness. And because of it.

Perfection is flawed

Have you ever felt like, no matter how hard you try, you're not good enough? We shy people set impossibly high standards for ourselves, which gives us the perfect excuse to hide. Cunning!

If nothing we do will ever measure up, there's not much point in trying. I'm plagued by the pressure of being the best. I used to make sculptures for fun. Except it wasn't fun. Whenever I made one, I expected that it had to be worthy of a solo exhibition. And when it wasn't? I'd have an artistic strop, smash it to pieces and flounce out of the room.

If nothing we do will ever measure up, what's the point in trying?

The pursuit of perfection gives us an excuse to dither and delay. Your painting is never quite completed. Your book is not ready to be read. Your project is not prepped for appraisal. Pursuing perfection can be paralysing.

If you're constantly criticising yourself and focusing on your flaws, waving scorecards, making lists of all your failings, the fear of messing up will dominate and lead you to do nothing.

And every time you drop the ball, or things go wrong, you come down on yourself like a massive skip-load of bricks. Perfection is too much pressure. It sets us up to fail.

It's *what you do* that counts – the difference you make, not the fact that you do it with perfect hair. Perfection is too perfect and sanitised and dull. It's like living life through a filter. That gets boring. It's not real. Aiming to be the person who goes to the gym and doesn't break a sweat. The person who emerges looking pristine. The person who sails through public speaking, without hesitation or nerves. The person who launches a business in one dramatic, doubt-free swoop. That's not real.

Why wait until every wobble is gone, we score a perfect ten or achieve world-champion status before we can be even a little bit pleased with ourselves? If we hold ourselves to such high account that we can only be proud of ourselves or think we did a good job when we're the best of the best, then I can tell you now, we'll never be happy. Withholding kindness until we reach perfection is painful.

We don't expect everyone around us to be perfect. In fact, we are good at being understanding of others. Of accepting their flaws. And yet, we expect nothing less than perfection when it comes to ourselves.

Embrace the mess

Last week, I wore a new black sweatshirt to the gym. I wore it to warm up in and then, when I got a bit boiling, I took it off. Unbeknown to me, I spent the rest of the session covered in black fluff, looking like a gorilla who'd forgotten to trim. At the end of the class, I popped to the loo and beheld the full extent of my fashion faux pas. I particularly loved how the black fluff had stuck to my armpits, making me look like I was making some kind of feminist style statement. I was mortified.

Part of me wanted to change gyms and never go back. I felt like everyone was laughing at me behind my back. Epic embarrassment.

But when I told my gym buddy what had happened, she confessed that the exact same thing had happened to her. We had a little chuckle about it. Decided to wash our new sweatshirts a few times before working out in them. And to check each other for fluff. Fluffy friends forever.

If we plotted the journey to mightiness on a graph – I do love a graph – it wouldn't be a straight, diagonal line. It would be wiggly and scribbly, with bigger loops than a rollercoaster. Mightiness is messy and lumpy. Things go wrong. We mess up. And that's just life. It's real. Sure, things are a lot less risky if we stay put on the sofa, but life under a blanket is also a lot less exciting.

What if you get covered in fluff? Does that mean you're never going to wear the sweatshirt again? Nope. Maybe you tried speaking up in a meeting and someone spoke over you, or you didn't really get your point across. Does that mean that meetings are now dead to you? Of course it doesn't; it just means that you didn't do so great that one time. But you'll have another go.

A wise man called Brian, my boxing coach, once said to me, 'We are all knobheads.' We are all a bit silly, messy and crazy at times. We're not perfect. We're not robots. We cock things up. We say the wrong thing. We find things challenging. We miss stuff. We wimp out. We're a big old mish-mash of traits. A jumbly mess. Good and bad. And that's ok.

Let's embrace all the rich messy, mucky, tangled aspects of being a real-life human person. It's a bit like trying to cram your curves into a pair of body-shaping knickers; if we try to smooth over the lumpiness of life, the lumps will just squidge out the sides, where we definitely don't want them.

Instead of hiding from our shyness, let's embrace it, and learn to laugh at it a little. If we can chill and stop comparing ourselves with others – wishing we were louder, more strident, more bullish – we could breathe, calm down and get on with living our lives. Only then, when we're fully embracing it, can we work with it, instead of wishing things were different.

Embracing our inner knobhead means acknowledging that some-times things don't go according to plan. The important thing is that you are not a total dick to yourself, and you can just move on from it.

Once we get that into our silly heads and realise that messiness is part of mightiness, we can get on with working on ourselves, working hard and working it.

My alter ego: a more mighty me

When I am at the gym, I am myself. But I am also a more mighty ver-sion of myself. It's like I have an alter ego, living deep down inside me.

In the gym, adorable, sweet and shy Nadia becomes Bad Nad.

Bad Nad is a more aggressive version of me. She is tough. Powerful. Ruthless.

Tapping into my Bad Nad alter ego gives me the strength and courage I need to push myself to the limit, to overcome pain and setbacks and to get on with it, without worrying about whether my bum looks big. (I mean, why can't boxing shorts be more flattering, seriously?)

Bad Nad doesn't hunch her shoulders and shuffle along, hoping to be invisible. Bad Nad goes for the knockout.

Bad Nad is invincible.

Who will your mighty me be? Do they have a name? What are their powers?

If you want to go from invisible to invincible . . . you're gonna need a cape! Turn your comfort blanket into a cape! No more being buried by your blanket for you. They are so last season. A cape? Now that's a look! A strong look!

Thanks, blankie for keeping me safe all this time. I appreciate it. But now it's time for me to lead a more mighty life.

You can always flip your blanket over back to the fleecy side when you need a rest. It's good to know the fleecy underside is there, to keep you safe. But for now, we are going to wear our capes slinky side up!

This is a new beginning. A time for you to step forwards, out of the shadows, into the spotlight of your life. To be in charge of how you experience life from now on. Wearing your cape gives you strength. It gives you the courage to show up, to speak up and to shine.

From the moment I put my boxing wraps on, Bad Nad is in the house. The gloves, the shiny shorts, the gumshield – it's all part of the ritual. Plus, I look awesome.

Having a signal to tell yourself that you're ready to tap into your mighty mindset helps you get into the zone.

Your cape could be the smart shoes you put on for a meeting, your lipstick, a tie, a special necklace. Anything that symbolises the mightier version of you.

I decided to start dressing up and try wearing this 'costume' and I found that it actually helped me to get over this stage fright a bit . . . It's very childlike, I guess, but I felt kind of invisible . . . I find that dressing up for the job helps me focus and feel strong.

Chelsea Wolfe, musician*

Reframe your fears

Feeling nervous means you care. Sports people and actors feel nerves before they perform; it helps them to elevate their performance.

But what if you're paralysed by your jangling nerves?

Have you ever noticed how some of the reactions we have when we are feeling shy are similar to those we have when we are excited? Racing heart, sweaty bits, trouble forming a sentence . . .

On fight night, I get so nervous. The moment I arrive and see the ring and the other fighters milling around, the adrenaline starts pumping. It's full on. I worry about so many things: looking silly, tripping, messing up, letting my coach down and getting hurt.

When we feel these feelings, we can choose to label them as us freaking out, crapping ourselves, signs of weakness. Or we can reframe our nerves as excitement.

Instead of flapping about in my fears, I tell myself: my heart is racing because I'm excited. I feel flippy because I'm excited. I can't concentrate on my trashy novel because I'm excited. I think I may pee myself because I'm excited.

---

* https://chelseawolfemusic.tumblr.com/post/61787748781/i-have-to-say-i-find-it-very-fitting-that-its

Pick a purpose

I remember once, I was about to step out onto the stage in front of hundreds of teenagers. I was there to talk about shy power. But I was nervous as hell. My heart was pounding out of my chest. I felt like grabbing my things and doing a runner out of the nearest exit.

One of the other speakers saw me glancing at the door. He came up and asked me if I was ok. I explained that I'm shy, and that I was feeling all the nerves.

He said to me, 'If you don't show up for them, how can you possibly change their lives?'

He was right. If I wimped out and didn't manage to get on the stage, the impact I might have would be precisely nothing. If even one person found what I was about to say helpful, then my feeling afraid would pale into insignificance. I realised that my purpose was to give shyness a voice. And every time I push through my fears and nerves and worries I am doing just that.

When we focus on our purpose, on a mission that is bigger than us, we can find the strength to act. Even if we can't do it for ourselves, do it for others.

What is your purpose? Why is it important – to you, to other people, or to the world – that you tap into your mighty mindset and you put your fears to one side? Maybe you want to help your family, support your local community, help kids build better futures. Maybe you believe in our right to do things differently, or you want to give people the opportunity to change their lives.

And that reason, right there, is why it's worth getting sweaty pits.

The reset button

Imagine you're playing a computer game. Pow! Man down. Man down! Guts spilling out everywhere. You dead. Dammit. Part of you probably wants to throw the console out the window and never play the damn game again. But, more likely what you'll do is hit the reset button and go again.

The bell signalling the end of round two sounded, and I headed back to my corner, shattered. I had just suffered a two-fisted assault that left me seeing stars. The game plan had gone awry; my opponent was a monster. Part of me was ready to just lie down and have a little nap. The other part of me just really wanted my mum.

Capitulating was not an option. Everything that just happened had happened. It was done. It was time to take it to the next level. My coach grabbed me by the shoulder. He reminded me that I have power. And that, although I felt tired, I still had loads left in my tank. I drank some water. Regulated my breathing and reset. I stood up and headed back out there. Let's go, champ. Beast mode.

Don't look back, or dwell on your disappointments or focus on your failings or pick at the scabs of your missed opportunities. Imagine you're playing a computer game.

Hit the reset button and get back at it.

Maybe you didn't speak in a meeting. Or you missed an opportunity to chat to someone new. Or you didn't shine in that competition. Or you scuttled off the stage.

It's okay. Hit the reset button and go again.

MIGHTY MISSION

Try this and become instantly more mighty!

My Mighty Mantra.
Words are powerful. What could you say to yourself? Choose a phrase that speaks to you, maybe something like this:

- 'I am strong and brave.'
- 'I can do hard things.'
- 'I've got this.'
- 'I'm making a difference.'
- 'I am mighty.'

Pick something and then try saying it over and over again to yourself, like a mantra, perhaps when you're facing a challenging situation.

CHAPTER 15

MIGHTY POWERS

Because I'm such a shy person, having to live it out loud in front
of everyone has made me a stronger woman, so much stronger,
that it's been a gift to me in a way.

Kim Basinger, actor*

Pacific Power had a problem. During snowy weather in the Cascade Mountains, in the US, snow would tumble down onto the power cables, and when it froze, the ice would weigh down and stress the cables until they snapped. The only solution the company had found was so ridiculous, my mind is actually boggled: they would send linesmen out into the mountains to climb the icy poles and shake the cables. By hand. Climbing an icy pole and hanging on for dear life while you shake a heavy cable, all the while being eyed up by famished and freezing big brown bears. Erm, no thanks.

You can imagine that this was not a popular job. Business-wise, it was not only slow, inefficient and risky, but it was also expensive. They needed a different solution. And fast.

---

* https://thecreativemind.net/using-your-high-sensitivity-personality-as-an-actor/

Nobody was able to come up with an answer. So the management team decided to do something radical. They brought together a team of randomers from within the business, including accountants, managers, juniors, the guys who climbed the cables and a couple of secretaries. And they held a brainstorm.

At first, it didn't go well.

During a break, one of the more outspoken linesmen was regaling the group with the tale of one of his many bear-related near-death experiences. Clearly, being up a pole did not protect you from bears.

In the spirit of embracing all the ideas, someone who perhaps had been adding a little something to their coffee piped up that if the bears liked climbing the poles so much, maybe they could be trained to shake the wires while they were up there. Things started to get more 'blue sky' as someone else suggested that all they would need to do is go round and put pots of honey up all the poles. Seriously?

The ideas were flowing; not all of them practical.

I mean, how would they get the honey on the top of the poles? Surely, they would have to climb the poles, anyway, to do that? And who on earth would want to be wandering around with pots dripping with honey, surrounded by salivating bears?

One of the secretaries was yet to speak. A quiet and reserved woman, this was her first brainstorm, and she was feeling shy. She sat quietly taking notes. Thinking. She closed her eyes and tried to breathe, letting her thoughts and ideas flow.

Another of the linesmen, clearly miffed with the whole brain-storming process (although probably enjoying the coffee and biscuits and being in the warm) said, 'You know all those fancy helicopters those fat cats in the front office fly around in all the time? Why don't we grab one of those and fly from pole to pole placing the honey pots on top just after an ice storm? That way the honey will be there when we need it, and, besides, it will do those fat executives some good to walk for a change.'

Everyone laughed. But still, there were no serviceable solutions.

Ding. The secretary had an idea. She wasn't sure if she should say anything. I imagine, she started shifting and shuffling in her seat (as you do when you've got a good idea). The person next to her probably wondered why she was fidgeting and then reassured her that, frankly, her idea couldn't be more bonkers than bears climbing poles for pots of honey.

At that point, maybe she had a little chuckle to herself and relaxed. She knew she was in a safe space, where no idea would be ridiculed, and she felt secure and supported. She took a deep breath and said, 'I was a nurse's aide in Vietnam. I saw many injured soldiers arrive at the field hospital by helicopter. The downwash from the helicopter blades was amazing. Dust would fly everywhere. It was almost blinding. I wonder if we just flew the helicopter over the power lines at low altitude, would the downwash from those blades be sufficient to shake the lines and knock the ice off?'

Silence. Nobody said a word. Everyone was thinking; the crunching of mental gears was almost audible. It could work!

The quietest person in the room had come up with the solution. A simple, yet effective solution that would save many lives and mountains of money. It was revolutionary.

Nowadays, all Pacific Power needs to do when the snow cascades over the mountains is fly helicopters at low altitude over the wires, and the wind they create clears the snow and ice. Nobody needs to dice with death or climb icy poles. Nobody gets frosty fingers and chilly toes. And no bears are involved.

You see. Shy people have powers.*

Let's change the story around shyness

If I can view my shyness as an attribute and not a handicap, then I can put it to one side and do great things.

Ollie

The traditional narrative around shyness has always been that it's a prison. It's difficult. It ruins our lives and holds us captive.

And sure, we all know that, at times, shyness can feel like we are being controlled by that bully who's locked the door, and has their sweaty hand firmly placed over our mouths. Shyness stops us from socialising, from saying what's on our mind and from being seen. And it often feels like our shyness places limitations on our possibilities, on our potential and our future.

I would never downplay how undeniably difficult the shy life is. Being shy is pretty shitty at times. However, I do think there are some positives.

I always feel I have to compensate for being quiet by being smarter or better at something than others. I love the idea of being able to surprise people with some talent or knowledge they might assume I didn't have because I don't brag about it loudly in the break room.

Theo

---

* Pacific Power story: http://dtinblack.github.io/creative-solutions/

Before writing this book, I hadn't ever thought about shyness as a strength. But once I started to delve deeper, it was amazing how changing the way we look at shyness is actually helpful. Given that we've all committed to embracing our shyness and trying to own it, it would be easier to do that if there were good things about it. Nobody wants to embrace something that stinks.

I like the way Joe Moran puts it in his book *Shrinking Violets*:* 'I have decided, as the software developers say, that being shy is a feature, not a bug.'

I like the idea that we shy people have secret strengths that we hold in reserve and unleash when the moment is right. Then, we can take over the world, ever so quietly – in fact, so quietly that nobody notices until it's too late. Mwah, ha, ha.

In some cultures, shyness is a strength

What if shyness was the ideal? In some cultures, shyness is regarded as a blessing. In Japan, for example, where 57 per cent of people are shy, shy people are considered to be modest, introspective, approachable and good listeners.

Japanese culture does not celebrate chitter-chatter. In the spirit of Samurai warriors, calm, silent reflection and deep thinking are held in high esteem. In Japanese folklore, heroes sometimes use *Ishin-denshin*, a silent method of communication, a bit like 'the force'.

Haya is an Arabic word that means 'natural or inherent shyness and a sense of modesty'. In Islamic culture, shyness is deemed

---

* Joe Moran, *Shrinking Violets*, Profile Books, 2016, p. 237.

to be an essential quality and branch of the faith, and something to aspire to.*

In Sweden, listening is linked with deep thinking, modesty and humility. Listening, rather than talking, is seen as a sign of good communication skills. Silence is a strength and people think carefully, choose their words precisely before opening their mouths. Those who talk too much, or talk for the sake of it, are seen as unreliable. And if you've ever seen Swedes waiting for the bus or train, it's clear that they're not keen on invading each other's personal space. They definitely didn't need a pandemic to start social distancing.

If these guys have sussed that there's a plus to shyness, then perhaps they're on to something. Let's delve a little deeper and see what mighty strengths and skills we can discover, lurking inside our shy selves.

We are humble

Look at me – I'm wonderful! Did I tell you about my myriad massive achievements? Did I mention my Instagram and the dazzling montage of me in a bikini, pouting at the camera, showing off my hot body and perfect lifestyle?

No, of course I didn't. Because shy people are humble. We don't go on about how fascinating or marvellous we are.

> I'm now middle-aged and have grown to be comfortable with how I am, but when I was younger, I found it all very embarrassing. At work, I do think it held me back in the first few years – at the time

---

* https://www.arabnews.com/node/321425

when you need to make an impression, I was very conscious that
people who were showier were assumed more talented or intelligent.
I then moved into a role that required in-depth thinking more than
showy talking and felt as if I came into my own.

Lee

Frankly, we're pretty crappy at accepting compliments and useless at bragging. We are modest. (Which, I suppose, does sound a bit like bragging, doesn't it?!) We don't waste time bigging ourselves up or playing games. We keep ourselves to ourselves. Basically, we are not total douchebags! And that's probably why we tend not to think of our shyness as a positive.

We think deeply

Stephen Hawking knew what he was on about when he said, 'Quiet people have the loudest minds.'

There are oodles of thoughts going on inside our shy brains. It's hardly surprising, given the amount of time we spend hanging out in our own heads.

Being quiet does not mean you are less knowledgeable or skilful.
Quiet guys create and analyse thousands of ideas in their minds
while listening. I have seen many people keeping mostly quiet in a
meeting but transforming the whole conversation constructively with
one single statement taking five seconds only.

Colin

We might say we think too much, that we go around and around our own heads, overthinking and worrying. It's not all negative thinking, though. We're also busy mulling, planning, imagining, solving, extrapolating, forecasting and generally pondering. If we were busting out the weights, working out our brain cells and exercising our synapses in the brain gym, we would be ripped, positively bulging.

Neither E = mc² nor Paradise Lost was dashed off by a party animal.

Winifred Gallagher, science journalist

All that ruminating and pondering means we think about things deeply, we weigh things up and we have a big imagination and lots of ideas swirling around our heads. We have a treasure trove crammed with ideas, wisdom, solutions, insight and gold, just waiting to be discovered. When we feel safe to speak up, we are worth listening to. It's why we are the silent potential.

We are creative

Cezanne was shy. Alan Bennet was shy. Dirk Bogarde was shy. L.S. Lowry was shy. Françoise Hardy was shy. Agatha Christie was shy. Lady Gaga is shy. Jarvis Cocker is shy. Beyoncé is shy. Shy people are creative and innovative. We are inspired.

As a teenager, J.K. Rowling was incredibly shy. Her shyness and insecurities were made worse by relentless bullying. Being called 'rowling pin' and being pushed around and attacked on a regular basis knocked the stuffing out of her. Joanne withdrew and became more and more reserved. To cope with her isolation and loneliness she learned to enjoy spending time alone and would spend hours reading and conjuring up stories and characters.

She continued to inhabit her wonder-filled imagination as an adult. And then, one day, she was travelling on a train, when, in true British transport style, it got stuck for four long, tedious, interminable hours. Staring out of the window at the bleakness, she set her thoughts free, running wild, until the seedling of an idea started to bubble and fizz, gather pace and percolate. Joanne was onto something special; she was sure of it. She had to write it down before, puff, her idea vanished in a whisper of smoke.

Only, she'd gone and forgotten her pen! Damn.

To my immense frustration, I didn't have a pen that worked, and I was too shy to ask anybody if I could borrow one . . . But I do think that this was probably a good thing. I simply sat and thought, for four (delayed train) hours, while all the details bubbled up in my brain . . .

J.K. Rowling, author*

Yeah, it's a lot. But I like to think of shyness as a gift. We are uniquely placed to be able to process more data than most people. Plus, we appreciate the little details that make us happy. We relish the little things that most people would just miss, or step over or take for granted.

---

* https://highlysensitive.org/resources-introverts-highly-sensitive-people/

We're born to write

Did you know that poet Emily Dickinson was so shy that she would talk to visitors from behind a door? She may as well have sat there with a paper bag over her head. And Agatha Christie was voted in as the Chairperson of the Detective Club but agreed only on the proviso that she would never have to do any public speaking.

We might not love the public speaking, interviews, book tours, launch parties or shmoozing, but the writing, now that's something we shy people were born to do.

When voicing our ideas is a challenge, expressing ourselves through words on a page is a gift. Writing gives us permission to rummage through the coffers of ideas and thoughts stockpiled in our minds. It enables us to take our time to think, hone our sentences, ponder, chew on a pencil, scrub things out, review and revise, before finally choosing to reveal our work to the world – or not.

When we write, there's no pressure to get things right the first time, as every word can be carefully chosen, every sentence carefully constructed. We can research, plan, primp and polish to our heart's content. Our love of depth and detail, description and observation is perfectly suited to the written word. Writing gives us a voice.

We are listening legends

Don't be so quick to talk ... Listen a while before you speak. Advanced Game.

Ice T, rapper

There's a trendy new idea among thought leaders that society needs to talk less and do more. How radical. Sorry – I just find this hilarious. Because we shy people have been doing this all along.

I listen well. And I really listen. Like, between the lines, understanding what people really mean, not just what they say. I think that is a rare and invaluable skill.

Stuart

Listening seems to have gone out of fashion. There is so much hot air being pumped out into the atmosphere. Everywhere we go, people are talking for the sake of saying something, attempting to stake their claim on the conversation. There is an epidemic of verbal diarrhoea. And when people just won't shut up, there's not a lot of listening or thinking going on. And when everyone is talking, nobody is listening. It's just noise.

When I started teaching a few years ago, I thought I had to be big and charismatic and amazing to succeed, but quickly realised that teaching needs quiet, stillness and is much more effective when I truly listen and give a voice to the people in front of me.

Bea

I actually have a friend who doesn't listen to a word I say. I think the last time she listened to me was in 2003. And yet, listening is what makes a conversation; it's what makes connections.

Putting a sock in it and taking a moment to listen is smart. Endless talking and blabbing is all about ego and showing off. When we listen, we learn. We notice things that other people miss. When we talk, we're chucking out sounds; that's the opposite of absorbing; it's expelling. And it can show a lack of restraint.

> *There is too much noise in our world right now. It is important to take time to reset, to breathe, meditate and learn to listen properly. We quieter, less confident folk are excellent listeners.*
>
> Norah

Shy people make good leaders and managers, therapists and counsellors because we hear what other people are telling us. We give other people space to speak, we pay attention to their needs, we encourage them, we think about what they've said, we learn and then we respond.

We may not be the loudest or the bossiest or most dominant person in a team, but we are important. As we saw earlier, it's been proven that teams with a mixture of people in them perform better. Teams with cognitive diversity. That means us too. Our voices matter.

> *I am naturally less of an extrovert than most other salespeople, and I've worked in a lot of environments where I was made to feel uncomfortable for not being 'loud'. But the best salespeople are always the best listeners. I've also worked for sales 'leaders' who thought that talking a lot meant that they were in control. When, in actual fact, they were probably less confident underneath, and less in control than the quiet one in the corner.*
>
> Audrey

We are cautious

Shy people are not the throw-caution-to-the-wind types. We don't rush in, waving our arms around, all guns blazing. We like to prepare for all eventualities, we take a moment to weigh up the risks, to listen to different perspectives and then we decide on a well-considered and properly planned course of action. We prefer to pause, plan and ponder the pros and cons before we pounce.

Shyness stops you from jumping into situations. A positive of being cautious is that you assess before action. I think I am more aware of others' feelings and am more intuitive because of it. And maybe a more empathetic person in general. I'm not sure the world values these traits as much as extroversion.

Chloe

If a herd of wildebeest headed our way, we would hide out in a cave and make a plan. We wouldn't make a rash decision, do something silly, put ourselves – or others – in danger, and end up getting trampled. We have survivability.

Therefore, in Darwinian terms, we have an evolutionary advantage. Perhaps the trait of shyness has survived so well because we're less likely to get eaten by lions or trampled by beasts. And because one way to keep warm under the blankets inside the cave is to work on reproducing.

Being cautious of hairy beasts and baddies from neighbouring tribes is a good thing. Being up for a scrap gets you killed. Hiding in the cave, looking after people, building booby traps or finding fun ways to keep warm is a smarter approach.

We get it done

Talking less means doing more. We shy people prioritise action over hot air. I'm sure we all know people who are filled with plans but never seem to implement their ideas. We know all about their ideas because they tell us. At great length. Endlessly.

I've met many people in management roles who have been loud and brash. Oftentimes, you know that's the only attribute that got them to that position. I grew up being taught to watch, listen and learn and have used that approach very well throughout my career. If you make a habit of delivering what you say you'll deliver, then you'll stand out on merit, not on the volume of your voice.

William

Words mean nothing without action and execution. And that's where we shy people excel. We just don't need to surround ourselves with a big PR machine, going on about our achievements.

The world needs do-ers.

I'm known as the second Director at work because I get things done. So if anyone wants anything achieved, they usually come to me.

Jane

We take time to think things through, we do our research, we work hard and get things done properly, to a high standard. We are diligent and dependable. We do a good job. We won't be standing at the water cooler chatting all day. We'll have our heads down, getting on with it. Doing the work.

We are loyal

We may find it hard to woo people with outlandish dance moves, snog a randomer at a bar or even approach and talk to someone we fancy – but once we have managed to meet someone or make friends, we keep them.

The fact that it can be tricky for us to get to know people means that we don't just chuck our friendship around like confetti. Our friends are valued and important to us. We may not have hundreds of them or be part of a massive gang. But the friends we have are really good ones. The bonds run deep. We cherish them and keep them close to us, for a lifetime.

We make people feel comfortable

We're not scary or aggressive towards people. We appear approachable. We are empathetic.

Shy people are sensitive to how other people are feeling. Lots of us shy bods are also highly sensitive people, also known as HSPs. Clearly, understanding our fellow humans is a good thing.

My quietness does make me mighty because I feel like I am approachable and warm to a lot of people who might feel overtaken by someone who is loud and outgoing.

Goran

We spend a lot of time wondering about other people's feelings. Do they like us? Are we acceptable? Will we fit in? All this thinking and empathising means that we are thinking about how other people think, and are tuned into their emotions. Therefore, we can conclude, in a highly scientific fashion, that we are not total dickheads.

> *Someone asked me to go to their parents' house and speak to them, to find out 'how the land lies'. She said she asked me because she thought the mother would listen to me and open up to me because of my quiet manner.*
>
>   Paul

Because you prefer the focus to be on other people and you care about other people, you're brilliant at helping and supporting other people. Other people will love the attention you give them, the fact you're sensitive to their feelings, you care what they think, and you're actually listening to what they're saying, and you want them to like you. OK, so some of this is needy on our part, but on the other hand, in many situations, being able to get on with others and take care of them is a good thing.

> *I realised I am mighty when mentoring volunteers. These were people unable to work, or the elderly. I coached them and nurtured them as equals in a friendly, professional way. I was mighty because I was gentle, empathetic and welcoming.*
>
>   Tina

We are mighty leaders

In June 2020, shy and quiet Manchester United footballer Marcus Rashford, a talented player on the field, became an unlikely gamechanger off the pitch.

At a time when he could have stayed at home, recovering from a double stress fracture in his back and shielding from Covid-19, the softly spoken twenty-three-year-old worked tirelessly in support of families who relied on free school meals.

When a blinkered Boris Johnson announced that these free meals, a lifeline for so many families, would be stopped during the summer holidays, Rashford wrote to the PM asking him to reconsider. He pleaded with the government to change their decision. 'This is about humanity,' he wrote. 'Looking at ourselves in the mirror and feeling like we did everything we could to protect those who can't, for whatever reason or circumstance, protect themselves.'

He explained that he himself had grown up in a challenging situation and had personal experience of soup kitchens and food banks. And when the government refused to listen, Rashford took swift action, to give these struggling families a voice. He started a one-man mission to persuade the narrow-minded government to extend free school meals during the pandemic, to ensure that no child would go hungry. He didn't shout or scream. There was no fanfare or PR machine. He simply stood up for something he believed in and kept working and pushing until he got what he wanted. He had a powerful vision, based on personal experience, and a desire to prevent any child having to go through the kind of hunger and poverty he did. This drove him forwards and gave him the strength he needed to stand up to cynics and critics.

When the press tried to undermine his campaign, and accuse him of hypocrisy, Rashford stood firm. He was calm and dignified.

It should not have come down to one lone twenty-three-year-old footballer to get the government to look after its poorest children, during a pandemic. But thank goodness he was there, to get them to face up to their responsibilities.

Shy power right there. Marcus Rashford didn't shout or scream. He stood up for what was right and for what mattered, quietly and with dignity. And when he was awarded an MBE by the Queen in 2021, he gave it to his mum. What a nice boy.

We're tough as nails

Shyness means navigating a world that was not built for us in mind. This makes me feel adaptable and open-minded to change in all aspects of my life. There's also never-ending growth with shyness and so many little victories that others may take for granted.

Levi

The fact that being shy has its challenges means you've probably had to push yourself harder to do things that other people find easy. All these things take courage and effort when you're a shy person. While the challenges you face can be bloody annoying, it also means you can cope with anything life throws at you. You're strong AF!

I was the little girl who was bullied, and now I am a senior software engineer. I have come a long way! I have overcome so many challenges, and while I often don't feel it, I am resilient, tenacious and determined.

Anna

Camila Cabello is a pop powerhouse. She's shifted millions of albums and shone brightly on the biggest stages. Camila is also a shy person who, for many years, was completely stymied by her shyness. As a little girl, Karla – as she was then known – found singing in front of people completely crippling. At home she could bang out a Beyoncé belter in her basement, but when it came to singing for her parents, she'd burst into tears, and when she attempted to audition for the school choir, nerves set in and she forgot the words.

But this kid was not to be beaten. She was determined to find a way to let her voice shine. When she finally got her big moment to audition in front of thousands, she introduced herself as Camila. Off the cuff, she created a more confident alter ego. A mighty version of herself.

Unlike Karla, Camila wasn't shy or nervous. And when she started to sing, she forgot about her fears and fell back in love with singing.

Since that moment, Camila hasn't looked back. She's worked and worked and worked and has become famous, not just for her singing, but for her special songwriting skills too. Her shyness seems to have helped her to manifest mighty powers.

Shyness makes you face things and deal with things. It can be scary, but the feeling of achieving something is amazing.

Isabella

We have magic inside us

It was very natural for me to want to disappear into dark theatre, I am really very shy. That is something that people never seem to fully grasp because, when you are an actor, you are meant to be an exhibitionist.

Nicole Kidman, actor

Thanks to the body positivity movement, society is starting to celebrate the beauty of difference in our bodies. And yet, when it comes to what's going on inside our heads – our cognitive preferences and personalities – we are meant to conform.

Being shy doesn't mean we are failed extroverts.

Just as oranges are not the only fruit, extroverts are not the only kind of person. And beyond that, they are not the only ones with skills.

> *I'm imaginative. I'm creative. It's a gift. I care more than others do, see more than others do. I've accepted this side of me. This is who I am. I love myself!*
>
> Aurora

We have skills in spite of our shyness, and . . . drum roll . . . we have skills *because* of our shyness.

There is magic inside us.

MIGHTY MISSION

Try this and become instantly more mighty!

- Make a list of your mighty powers – the skills and strengths you have because you're a shy person.

CHAPTER 16

MIGHTY MUSCLES

Above all, be the heroine of your life, not the victim.
Nora Ephron, writer and journalist

Pandamonium

I love pandas. They're all cute and cuddly and roly-poly. And they know the impact of a monochrome outfit. I admire how chilled out they are, and the fact that they can pee up a tree in a handstand position, without getting wee all over themselves. Very impressive.

These fuzzy flooffers are the epitome of high maintenance. They need to eat 40 lbs of bamboo every day just to survive. That's a lot of bamboo! And they get to spend 14 hours a day sitting around stuffing their furry faces. Not too shabby.

Pandas are very specific. They like what they know, and they know what they like. They've got us humans running around after them, panda'ing to their every whim.

I wish I was more like a panda (apart from the being endangered part and the being too lazy to have sex part). I'd like to be specific and fussy and stamp my furry paws to get what I want.

Not made for us

In the country I grew up and spent much of my career in, being quiet is still seen as a weakness. An excuse for not being well prepared. Or worse, a reason to get picked on. The loudest man wins on our roads, and in our boardrooms. The truth is that this culture prevails across much of the developing world and isn't going to change any time soon.

Malik

We shy people are living in a world that is not made for us, because it's not made by us.

Our voice is missing from the conversation. We are not sitting at the table. And often, we are not even in the room; we're just lurking outside. As a result, we end up existing in an outgoing society that has been designed by a bunch of loud, gregarious, extrovert world-architects with a penchant for showing off.

From the moment we enter the education system, we struggle to find a voice. And it continues throughout our lives.

I struggle with classrooms because all of the loud people always ask the teacher questions and I'm scared to ask the teacher anything because the loud people are taking up all of the teacher's time. I would like everyone to be quiet, doing their work instead of talking.

Brielle

If you want to shine at school, you'd better be good at speaking in front of the class. If you want to play professional sport, you'd better get used to courting the media.

If we're not comfortable speaking up in front of a crowd, bigging ourselves up and raising our profile, it seems like we're going to falter and fumble. Extroversion is built into everything; it's the foundation, the bricks and the cement of our society. It's irksome, isn't it? If only things were easier. More suited to our way of thinking and being.

Society is not designed for small voices. Loud people who are not good at listening are the norm. I think a general rethink in society to value kindness, calm and respect would help, but that's a big ask!

Alex

We're not being very panda, are we? And you know what makes this whole situation worse? Not only are we living in a world where we don't feel like our faces fit, we've also handed control over to a bully. Our shyness.

We've allowed our shyness to dictate how we spend our time, who we talk to, when we talk, the words we say. Our shyness has silenced our potential.

Where did you go?

For a long time, I went along with what other people wanted to do. I couldn't be bothered to argue, stand up for my own opinions or have a big discussion. So, I just put up and shut up.

I would go see people I didn't want to see. Get roped into obligations I didn't want. Go to places I didn't like. Eat food I didn't want to eat. Agree to things I didn't agree with. Keep my mouth and my feelings zipped up. And nod along, like one of those toy dogs people have in their cars.

Putting your needs aside, surrendering control and just wafting along is easier than expressing your desires. It's easier than having a conversation or standing up for yourself.

Until it isn't.

Until you start to feel very cross indeed. When you find you don't actually know what you want any more.

I don't mean to sound like a drama queen, but one day, I realised I had no real clue what I actually liked or wanted. I had become so used to not using my voice that I'd lost it. Somewhere along the way, I had lost myself.

Use it or lose it, as they say.

Be more boss

In the movie, *The Holiday* (which I have seen about 400 times), Arthur Abbot, a celebrated screenwriter, says to his new neighbour: 'Iris, in the movies, we have leading ladies and we have the best friend. You, I can tell, are a leading lady, but for some reason, you're behaving like the best friend.'

She replies, 'You're so right. You're supposed to be the leading lady of your own life for god's sake!'

Stand down, shyness! It's time for a change. It's time for us to step forwards into the light and take back control of our lives. We're taking back our power. It's a coup. A very quiet coup.

Who says things have to be done the way they are done? Who says that the other 50 per cent of the population get to dominate us and boss us around? Who says that only the loudest voices get a say? Who says that only the most outgoing people get to decide how things are done?

Instead of allowing stuff to happen to us or trying to fit in with everyone else, instead of being a victim to our circumstances, let's think about what we need and what works for us. And then, let's create it.

No more letting people talk over us. And for us. And instead of us. No more being overlooked. And underestimated. We can shape the world around us. We can create the conditions that work for us. We don't have to squidge ourselves into this loud way of living that squashes and silences us.

We are powerful and brave, and unique and mighty. We can do this.

Your mighty moment

Shy, bullied and severely overweight, Lawrence Okolie was grinding it out in McDonald's, in the summer of 2012, dreaming of a better life.

Taking a break from flipping the burgers to eat the burgers, Lawrence slumped down in a tiny, rickety chair in the breakout room and flicked on the TV. The Olympics were on. It just so happened that right at that moment, Anthony Joshua was boxing for the gold medal.

Fists were flying. It was a close fight. Lawrence leaned forwards, enthralled, living every slip, roll and punch as if he were right there in that ring.

When AJ raised his arms, victorious, a wave of hope rippled across London and engulfed Lawrence Okolie. It was the split second that would alter the course of his life for ever: the moment he chose a different, more daring path. His mighty moment. He decided that in four years' time, he would be fighting at the 2016 Olympics. Despite the fact that he was not a boxer. Despite the fact that he was overweight. Despite the fact that he had no idea how to get there. Talk about a big-hairy-ass goal.

We all have the power within us to move forwards. We are not frozen in a block of ice or set mafia-style in a slab of concrete. If we want to make a change, we can. It's as simple as that.

> *If you're telling yourself that there's nothing special about you, as if that's a reason for not doing anything with your life, I'm telling you that no one's special. We all have the power within ourselves to push and do great things. You just have to get that ambition out. You might think that you don't have the ability or the drive to do something with your life, but that's probably because you've never tried before.*
>
> Lawrence Okolie, boxer

It comes down to a decision. Do you want to progress? Or do you want to stay exactly where you are now? Decision made.

Lawrence resolved to change his life. And he did. In just four years, he made it to the Olympics. And he's now a face-smashing, belt-winning professional boxer – as well as an author, rapper and entrepreneur.

Let this moment – right here, right now – be your AJ-at-the-Olympics, life-changing moment. The story you'll tell your grandkids. The moment when you decided to go from invisible to invincible. Your mighty moment.

Go big or go home

American novelist Jonathan Safran Foer wrote, 'Shyness is when you turn your head away from something you want. Shame is when you turn your head away from something you do not want.' When we feel shy, we turn away from the thing we want. We become unaccustomed to having a goal and going after it.

We have big dreams, which expand with hope and optimism. Dreams energise us and give our lives meaning and direction. If we know what we desire, we can go after it. Sometimes, though, our shyness stops us from taking action. It makes us feel trapped, and we don't even give ourselves permission to dream. Perhaps we feel like it's childish or indulgent. Or perhaps we feel like we are not capable of achieving big things.

Our shyness is like a pesky pin prick, causing the big balloons of our dreams to deflate and shrivel up, until they lie flaccid and defeated on the floor.

Don't let shyness deflate your dreams. Your goals and desires matter. They are vital. They are significant.

Be audacious in your aspirations. Close your eyes for a moment and let your mind wander. What do you really want to be doing in, say, five or ten years' time? What will your life be like? Who do you want to surround yourself with? How do you want to spend your days? How will you feel when you are there? Take your time and let the pictures form in your mind.

Now, open your eyes. And bring to mind what you saw.

No matter how ambitious, exciting or unusual, you can do this. You *will* do this.

It's as simple as that.

Commit to it

Shy actor Jim Carrey was flat broke. But, not satisfied with struggling along, scraping around for scraps of work, he set his sights on a cool $10 million. He committed to it, by writing himself a cheque.

I wrote myself a check for $10 million for 'acting services rendered' and I gave myself five years . . . or three years, maybe. I dated it Thanksgiving 1995 and I put it in my wallet and I kept it there and it deteriorated and deteriorated. But then, just before Thanksgiving 1995, I found out that I was going to make $10 million on Dumb and Dumber.

Jim Carrey, actor*

As soon as Lawrence Okolie made the decision to become a boxer, he started chatting about it as if it were a certainty. Putting his vision out there into the real world kept him focused and accountable to himself and his dream. The fact that people knew what he was working towards meant that if they really cared about him, they would cheer him on and support and encourage him on his journey. Plus, they were more likely to understand when he needed to train all the hours, get to bed early, eat crazy amounts of protein and, erm, abstain from sex before a fight.

Let's all commit to our goals too. Write them down, say them out loud and share them with the people we trust. Put them out there and make them public, so we don't have to keep explaining ourselves, and we can't give up or get distracted.

And then, we can get to work making them happen.

Find the fun

When you're thinking about where you want your life to go, and how you'll become more mighty, find something you actually like.

---

* https://www.cheatsheet.com/entertainment/why-jim-carrey-wrote-himself-a-10-million-check-before-he-was-famous.html/

If my chosen path was to become a pole dancer, I would fall at the first hurdle. There is nothing about pole dancing that appeals to me. Gripping a pole with your thighs, wearing just a bikini, having to hold positions with pointy toes, being graceful and getting bruises in private places. Stop it!

You're more likely to keep working on something if it's fun. If it's agonising and tedious, you won't wanna do it. Pretty obvious, really.

Considering this thing is now entrenched into your life, it should be something you actually like doing. There has to be an upside. We're not aiming to leave one dark, depressing prison and head for some kind of torture chamber, where we're regularly subjected to having our toenails extracted or something horrible like that.

I like boxing. I adore it. Which is why I can commit to it and work hard at it. I want to do it. Every day. It makes me feel good. The thwack of gloves against pads, or someone's face is kind of lovely. Call me weird, but it's brilliant.

The more fun you have being mighty, the more likely you are to keep doing it.

Break it down

Writing a book with thousands and thousands of words is a long and intense process. It's daunting, and I'm not sure I'm actually cut out for it!

Attempting to write a good book, with good-quality ideas and proper long words, is even harder. And, erm, attempting to write a decent book that people actually want to buy and enjoy reading feels impossible. It's paralysing.

A big ambition or goal can be scary. Instead of moving forwards and taking action, the gigantic goal mountain casts a shadow upon us and keeps us frozen in fear and overwhelms us, so that we can't move.

Talking of mountains ... When we were kids, my dad would always return from his business trips with stacks of Toblerone chocolate – you know, the Swiss, mountain-shaped, nougaty bars of chocolatey deliciousness. It was tradition. We were always happy to see him, but we were even happier to wedge giant bars of chocolate into our faces.

And I learned a valuable life lesson from that chocolate.

The only way to eat giant Toblerone? One chunk at a time.

If you try to conquer the whole thing in one go, you will break your face and all your teeth.

And so it is with our mighty goals. We have to break them down into bite-size chunks, so we don't freak out and get completely stuck. Because sometimes, where we are now and where we want to be seem like two points on a map that are impossibly far apart.

If your goal is to fight at the Olympics, what are the smaller targets you could set yourself to get there? Look at the journey and pick out some key milestones. Perhaps your first goal is to learn the basic punch combinations and have your first sparring session. After that, your next goal might be to sign up for your first amateur fight. And so it goes, step by step, until you reach the Olympics.

The famous app 'Couch to 5K' has helped thousands and thousands of people go from lazing around on the sofa in their underwear to running 5K and beyond. A guy called Josh Clark created it because he wanted to help his mum get active and start running too. For someone who doesn't run, the idea of running 5K seems like an insurmountable task. Newbie runners often feel bewildered and overwhelmed. They don't know where to begin. They risk going way too fast too fast and ending up with unmentionable injuries. Or just giving up when the going gets tough.

But when you break the goal down into smaller, more achievable goals, like being able to run for one minute at a time, then five minutes three times a week for nine weeks, gradually building up, you see real progress. And there's nothing more motivating than making progress.

The fact that it's all planned out means that you don't have to wonder what to do each day. It's all decided for you. The guesswork has been extracted from the equation. There's less scope for whingeing, wimping out or throwing in the sweaty gym towel. The system has been designed to help you take consistent action towards the ultimate goal of running 5,000 whole metres without stopping for a sit-down, a bacon sarnie and a full-fat latte.

Breaking your goal down into mini mighty milestones does not detract from your dream. You will still run a marathon. Or fight at the Olympics, make a million, or give that very impressive presentation. You will still eat the whole bar of Toblerone. The point is to make the process more manageable.

The feeling of achievement you'll get when you reach each mini mighty milestone will keep you going through the ups and downs and twists and turns of your journey. Reaching goals is motivating; it makes you feel good and builds confidence. Plus, you might even get some gold stars, stickers or prizes along the way. Yay!

Let's all give ourselves the chance of having that lovely feeling more often.

Baby steps

I am quite shy and I also like to do things where I have a little time to think about what I'm saying first.

Robert Pattinson, actor*

Shy people tend to take a little longer to warm up in new and uncertain situations. And pushing ourselves forwards towards our goals is, by definition, new and uncertain. So, let's lean into the fact that we prefer a slow and steady approach. We don't want to pull a muscle or do ourselves a mischief. Launching ourselves into full-on panic-inducing situations does not a happy shy person make. I'm sure we've all been shoved into things we didn't want to do, and still bear the scars to this day. So, let's not do that. We're not aiming to scare the living daylights out of ourselves, so that we never want to even try again.

Take it gradually. Set your sights on your first milestone and then break it down into teeny tiny baby steps, figuring out the manageable, mini things you need to accomplish along the way to your first milestone.

I'm not mighty yet. But I could be.

Tilly, age nine

Please pass me a Kleenex.

I didn't rock up at the boxing gym ready for a fight. Very far from it. I didn't even think about the prospect of fighting. If I had, I wouldn't have dared heave open the door to the gym. Believe me,

---

* https://www.digitalspy.com/showbiz/a305524/robert-pattinson-im-a-shy-person/

I did spend quite some time sat in the car before I actually entered the building.

At times the end goal is way too daunting to even contemplate. So, rather than worrying about the formidable and terrifying end result, start small. Like, really, really small. What are the teeny tiny little things you need to do to get to your goal?

A boxing gym seemed like such a masculine, alien environment. I was not representative of the usual clientele. I felt like I was too old, too fat, too unfit and too wimpy and weak to be there. Going to the group classes seemed like a total no-go. I mean, I had no experience, and what if I was mortifyingly terrible and nobody wanted to be my partner?

I was making limiting decisions and assumptions based on my own insecurities. But I really wanted to go, so I had to find a way to build up to it.

I knew my first milestone was to be able to attend the group boxing classes without feeling too self-conscious. And to get there, I took lots of small baby steps.

I warmed up by doing one-to-ones with a coach for a few months, to build my fitness and my skills, so I could survive a full hour of boxing without collapsing in a heap. I needed to learn the basic punches and how to put them together. And I had to learn the names of things, so I would know what was going on. When I felt like I was good enough not to look like a total tool, I felt able to go to the classes. Also, by then I knew my coach and a few other people, so I felt less afraid about rocking up there.

I admit I take a while and a lot of steps to reach each of my mini mighty milestones. To an outgoing, strident person these steps might seem silly, slow or pointlessly small. They are not.

Taking consistent little steps forwards to building your mightiness is the equivalent of nibbling away at each chunk of Toblerone. (Other massive chocolate bars are available, and this chapter is not sponsored by Toblerone – although if they did want to send me a lifetime supply, I would not be averse to that.)

As long as your baby steps are moving you forwards, and you feel like you're making progress, small is sensible. For example, let's say your goal is to be able to handle networking events. You start by aiming to make it through the door, then perhaps stay for half an hour. But if two years later you are still just showing up and chatting to the two mates you came with, that's a bit of a cop-out. Baby steps are not an excuse for paralysis. We need to challenge ourselves just enough. It's a careful balance, and only you know how much to push yourself.

Comfortable courage.

Our journey to becoming more mighty is a steady one. No big shocks or pain or drama. The key is to simply keep moving forwards and keep taking action and tiny risks, consistently, in the direction of your big goal. Until you get there.

Mighty habits

We are what we repeatedly do. Excellence, then, is not an act, but a habit.

Aristotle, philosopher

Mightiness is a habit. Like brushing your teeth, drinking enough water, washing your clothes or going to the gym.

According to research, it takes anywhere from two to eight months to form a habit. But once a habit is in place, it sticks. And almost without us noticing, it gradually builds in a stealth-like fashion, into something really impactful. Doing 100 squats a day for 100 days leads to buns of steel. Writing a page a day for 200 days leads to a book. Devising one line of code a day for 300 days leads to a computer game. Little habits, repeated daily, or regularly, build up to something big and brilliant, over time.

Take *the first* step

There's a whole world out there. A world of infinite opportunities, fun, excitement, success and recognition, just waiting for you.

Off you go then, go get it!

Eeek. Where to start?

We all have to start somewhere. The important thing is to actually start.

The lure of the sofa is strong. I know. I understand. And it's ok to rest and snuggle. We need to feel safe and snug and warm and fuzzy, sometimes. The trouble is the call of comfort can be stronger than the desire to become more mighty, and you end up getting stuck on the sofa under a smelly blanket for longer than is strictly hygienic.

And sure, there's no risk, coddled in your blankie. Nobody can get near you. You're safe and free from judgement and criticism. But there's no reward either. It's a very small existence. And you end up kind of festering in a semi-comatose state. With a box of pizza balanced on your stomach. And crumbs where there shouldn't be crumbs.

And we all know how hard it is to actually hoik yourself up off the sofa once you've spent ages there, lolling around. You end up kind of plopping onto the floor and landing in a heap. Not very stylish.

So, what's the solution? Give in to the sofa? Do nothing? Nope.

Do something? Anything? Yep.

The first step is the hardest. Making the decision to enter the competition. Downloading the job description. Replying to the invitation. Smiling at someone. Putting your ice skates on. Sending the text. Booking the first lesson.

Start small. But start!

Whether you want to start speaking up in meetings, or land a promotion, or get back on the dating scene, or start singing in a band, take the first step.

And then, after that, you'll take the next step. And the next.

What will your first step be?

Do the work

Everyone is shy – it is the inborn modesty that makes us able to live in harmony with other creatures and our fellows. Achievement comes not by denying shyness but, occasionally, by setting it aside and letting pride and perspiration come first.

Kirkpatrick Sale, author

There's a saying in boxing – 'Train hard, fight easy'. It's pretty self-explanatory. Do the damn work!

Think of working with your shyness and becoming more mighty as building your bravery muscles. If you wanted to get a peachy bubble butt, abs of steel, or massive pecs, you're gonna need to get your ass down the gym. And get to work. Regularly. And gradually, bit by bit, you'll build those muscles until you're totally ripped and busting out of your clothes!

Training is gruelling. All that skipping. All those rounds. All that running. All that grunting. And sweating. It's a grind. But boxers don't moan or whine. They just get on with it. Well, if they want to succeed, they do. There are no shortcuts.

This isn't some extreme mightiness makeover where we emerge from behind a curtain totally revamped, looking like a rather more plasticised version of ourselves. There's no magic pill or extreme veneers. I can't wave a wand and transform you into a bombastic bombshell with one quick swish and some gobbledygook.

And why would you want that anyway? We're embracing our shyness, remember. We're owning it. So, you don't want a full-frontal lobotomy, right?

When you're building your mighty muscles, you need to commit to being consistent. The temptation is to start something, have a bit of a bash at it and then dwindle off. In fact, that's what most people do when they're trying to achieve a goal.

Four visits to the gym in a year won't make a difference. Working on your mighty muscles a couple of times here and there will achieve precisely nothing. Which, of course, gives you the perfect excuse to stop trying.

Without hard work and commitment, you're setting yourself up to fail. You don't need to be more outgoing, or more confident, or luckier or a different person to succeed in your mission to mightiness. You are perfect just as you are. You just need to do the work.

If you want to develop your mighty muscles and become shy and mighty, you have to take little steps, pretty much every day. Until it's part of your life. Until your body and brain know what to do, intuitively. Like mighty muscle memory.

Most people won't bother or make the effort. Most people will come up with all kinds of crappy excuses to justify their lack of effort. They will be put off by the fact that results take time. And that they are not instantly transformed, like an Instagram tuning app.

But that's not you. You are not most people. You are shy and mighty.

You're committing to yourself; you're putting yourself first. Taking responsibility for your results. And prioritising your needs. You understand that progress takes time. And all that matters is your dedication to yourself and to your mightiness.

Mightiness is your life now. So, we need to do the work to back that up. Mightiness is inside you. It's who you are. And as someone who is shy and mighty, this is what you do. Simple.

Don't give up

My first sparring session freaked me out. (Sparring is like a practice fight, where you punch each other, but you're not meant to be trying to take each other's heads off.) For all the pad work and bag work I had done, I had never been hit before. Like, actually punched in the face. (I don't think that's particularly surprising, really, is it?)

It was alarming. And the more I panicked, the more I got hit. I felt really overwhelmed and couldn't seem to get out of harm's way. I wasn't getting hurt, but the punches were too fast and powerful and I felt like I couldn't breathe.

I wanted to cry. Part of me felt like jacking the whole thing in and never doing it again, perhaps taking up a more serene sport, like embroidery.

The truth is, there was no way I was going to be good at sparring the first time I tried. I had never done anything like it before. But, still, I wanted to run away and hide in the loo – probably for at least a week, when I would creep out, in the middle of the night, make my way home, and never speak of it again.

I had a choice. Bottle it and give up, or carry on and get better. I talked to my coach, and we figured out what had gone wrong. We spent time making sure I could handle that kind of pressure more effectively and we looked at improving the things that weren't working. (Fairly fundamental stuff, erm, like blocking shots and moving out of the way!)

When we try something once and it's difficult, it's not a reason not to try again. There will be no woe is me, flouncing off, feeling sorry for ourselves. Not on my watch.

When we put too much pressure on ourselves and a single interaction to be perfect, it gives us the ideal get-out clause. But, if we decide it's game over when things get a little sticky, we'll end up doing nothing at all. You can see how this kind of thinking leads to us staying at home under a blanket.

When things go wrong, the important thing is to learn from what happened and move forwards.

Dishevelled hair, sweaty bits, a bruised ego and the odd nosebleed are not reasons to take to your bed and never leave the house again.

Eat the ice cream

When things go well, accept that you were mighty. Bask in your glory. Admire your work. And most definitely celebrate with cake and ice cream. As soon as this chapter is finished, that's what I shall be doing.

We deserve the good stuff. We are magnificent in our mightiness, and yet our tendency is to belittle our achievements. We brush off our successes and assume that they only kinda happened by accident or because someone else did something, or there were all kinds of other random factors at play that had nothing to do with us.

If we connect with someone ravishing at a party, we assume they're only talking to us out of pity or to get to our friends. If we are selected for an award at work, we put it down to a mistake, some kind of oversight or the fact that someone else didn't show up. If we get nice comments about our work, we play them down. I know I do. I also pull a kind of grimacing face, and blush and go all silly. I tell people it's not a big deal, that it could have happened to anyone.

Except that *it is a big deal*. We are lovely and talented and we are doing big, brave things. We are worthy of praise.

Shouting it from the rooftops, hiring a brass band, commissioning a cheerleading squad or getting a plane to write our names in the sky might not be our style. But when we achieve great things, let's revel in them, even for a minute or two. Let's bask in the glory of our success.

Quietly, of course.

MIGHTY MISSION

Your final mighty mission is to commit to taking the first step.

We have a tendency to overthink and get stuck in our own heads, worrying about what people will think, or if we'll be good enough and all that stuff. But not today. Today, you're going to take the first step towards becoming shy and mighty. Your first step can be tiny, really tiny. The key is action.

- Step 1: Write down your first step.
- Step 2: Put this book down.
- Step 3: Go and DO IT.

TOP TIPS

Socialising and dating

- **Old and new** We feel shy in new and uncertain situations, so be sure to balance this out with familiar things: suggest going somewhere you've been before; wear something you've worn lots of times; take the route you're most familiar with. Getting to know a new person is enough newness for one day.

- **Help out** Peopling with a purpose helps us to squish our fears. Volunteer in your local community, help in a school, work in a charity shop, run a bake sale. Focusing on *doing* good will do *you* good, too.

- **Eyes and ears** Select socialising methods that can be enjoyed in silence and switch on your other senses. Watch a movie. Go see a band. Visit a gallery. And when the show is over, you'll have plenty to discuss.

- **Take precautions** Before you head out and about, get strategic. Eat something in case you have a little too much to drink. Spray on some decent deodorant. Choose comfy clothes and shoes that are not likely to malfunction. Wear dark colours that don't show sweat patches. If you're prone to blushing, wear a high neckline. Plan ahead to reduce the risk of fallout. Or falling out. Or falling over.

- **Friend zone** If you're worried about stepping out onto the scene all on your lonesome, then don't. Bring a buddy along with you or another couple if you're going on a date. Choose wisely, though. Pick people you're super comfortable with, who have your best interests at heart and who understand how to help you shine.

- **Take comfort** Make yourself feel safe and snug when you're socialising. A woolly blanket may be a step too far, but tactile fabrics, furry boots, a cashmere scarf, a fluffy sweater or your favourite jacket will help you relax and give you a sense of wellbeing.

- **Shy alert** You won't be the only shy person in the room. Look out for other shy people standing alone, lurking at the edge, propping up the bar, hiding in the kitchen . . . Seek them out – you know the signs, after all – and go be awkward together. You'll both be so glad you did.

- **Open up** Think about your body language. Uncross your arms, don't slouch – and, for goodness sake, smile. When you appear open, welcoming and happy, people are more likely to come and talk to you.

- **Be curious** If you're not sure what to say, ask away instead. Ask open questions. People love to talk about themselves and their passions. So rather than worrying about what to say next, or if you're doing the whole talking thing right, really listen to what people are saying. And, then, just ask more questions. Just don't get too intense; we're aiming for attentive here, not the Spanish Inquisition.

- **Pay attention** Focus on the person you're with. Show them that you care about them having a good time. Give them your full attention, make them feel comfortable and ensure they have everything they need. Show them that they are important to you.

- **Expect mess** Life is not much like a fairy tale; things do go wrong. Wine gets spilled. Spaghetti is difficult to eat in polite company. We all trip over our feet sometimes and stand on other people's. Get ready to laugh at yourself and embrace the fact that relationships are messy and when two people collide, they often do.

- **A quiet word** If you're keen to go and talk to someone new, wait for a quiet moment – perhaps when they're on their own, or walking away from a group. It's harder to approach people when they're with their friends or in the middle of a conversation.

- **Look and look away** Prolonged eye contact can feel uncomfortable and awkward. But the good news is that we're not aiming for a staring contest here. The idea is to make eye contact for a moment, smile and then look away. Cute. And if you feel nervous or you blush or your words get a bit stuck, don't panic. These are normal reactions when you're with someone you like.

- **It's better to know** If you ask someone out and they say no thank you, don't assume it's because you're a total loser who will never get anyone. It could just be that the spark wasn't there. Or they're not looking to date right now. It's better to know this now than get messed around and find out way down the line.

- **Remember your mighty powers** You have skills that make you an excellent partner. You tune into the other person. You listen. You care. You are considerate. The ability to talk endlessly and fill every gap with witty banter is not the most important thing in a relationship.

- **Ease in gently** Most of us are shy around people we don't know well. But as you get to know people, you'll start to feel at ease. So, remember that even though you might feel shy at first, as your relationship develops, you'll feel more and more comfortable. Your feelings of shyness around them won't last for ever.

- **All of you** Your kind of people will love you for who you are. They will love all the different things about you, including your shyness. Don't mask your true self. Your honesty just makes you even more adorable.

Job interviews

Preparing for your interview

- **Dissect the job description** The key to success lies in understanding what the employer is looking for. And that is all in the job description. Put your mighty analysing skills to good use and try to draw out each of the skills they are looking for. List them, then work out which of your experiences and successes relates to each one. Try to find a few examples for each skill, which you can discuss when asked.

- **Dig deep** Find out as much as you can about the company in advance of your interview. Look at their recent successes, trends in the industry, as well as challenges which may be affecting the company. Check out any relevant recent reports, white papers, publications as well as trade journals, articles and press coverage. Demonstrating that you know your stuff shows commitment, preparation and deep thinking – all things that you're great at!

- **Answer me this** Think through all the interview questions you've been asked in the past, and what do you notice? They're kinda similar. Why do you want to work for us? What's your biggest weakness? Where do you see yourself in five years' time? Yada yada yada. Prepare responses to these classic questions, so you don't get caught out.

- **Portfolio** If you tend to freeze or get embarrassed when asked about your achievements, why not take a professional portfolio along to your interview to give you a calm confidence on the day? Prepare a one-page summary for the front of the folder with a brief description of your five to ten main professional achievements. Behind your summary sheet include examples of your work, case studies, awards or reviews which are relevant to the job. Being able to talk through your achievements without getting embarrassed or having a temporary brain block makes it easy for you to – literally – show your interviewer how amazing you are.

- **Final thoughts** You know they're going to ask you if you have any questions at the end of the interview – so prepare some. Be ready with at least five questions (either in your mind or written neatly on a card), making sure they are relevant to the organisation. No awkward silences or winging it for you.

- **Dry run** Practise your interview technique with a friend you can trust – someone who knows what they're doing and has time to go through a full interview with you a few times. Take it seriously, though; no mucking around. Get them to ask you questions and practise giving your answers.

- **Dress for success** Plan your outfit ahead of time, so you're not panicking on the day. Go for something smart, which feels like you and is comfortable. Check you can sit down easily, and without revealing too much of anything. And steer well clear of colours that show sweat patches. No pale blue shirts, under any circumstances. If wearing a tie or heels makes you feel more powerful and confident, then wear them. Make sure everything is washed and ironed, ready for the big day. Don't forget the little things. Polish your shoes. And your nails. You want to look like you've made an effort.

- **Journey planning** To avoid any last-minute panics or traffic debacles, work out the best way to get to the interview, allowing loads of spare time, just in case. The goal is to avoid delays and stress, so that you arrive there early, cool, calm and collected.

- **Emergency kit** Nothing must derail you. You want to be more prepared than a boy scout. So pop a spare pair of tights or a tie in your bag, just in case you have a mishap. Take plasters if you're worried your shoes might rub. A spare phone charger. A bottle of water. A packet of tissues. Think ahead. If you've got all your risks covered, you can focus on dazzling in the interview.

On the big day

- **Be early** In the spirit of avoiding a mad panic, aim to arrive at the venue early. Give yourself a good few minutes to chill out, get used to the environment, gather yourself and your thoughts and make yourself comfortable.

- **Breathe for calm** Remember to breathe. While you're waiting and during the interview, you can use your breath to calm yourself and steady your voice. If you feel yourself panicking before the interview, try breathing in for 5 or 6 and out for 5 or 6 to regulate your breathing and bring about a sense of serenity. If you feel stressed before you answer a question, be sure to take a deep breath before speaking. This will help you to gather your thoughts and avoid rambling. Remember – your brain and body need oxygen to function.

- **Sit tall** Good posture gives the impression of confidence. If you lean back in your chair with your arms folded, you'll look like you're not bothered and don't want the job. If you slump down in your seat, with your shoulders hunched, you'll look nervous and lacking in confidence. Imagine a thread running through the top of your head up towards the ceiling, holding your spine straight and making you taller. Lean in towards the interviewer to show them you are engaged in the conversation and you really want the job.

- **Real rapport** Clearly, staring intently at your hands during the interview is more comfortable than looking your interviewer in the eye. However, if you're going to bag the job, you'll need to build a connection. The goal is to show that you're a friendly kind of a person, who knows how to get on with people, is interested in what they're saying and is happy to be there – and that is done by making eye contact and smiling from time to time. If it doesn't come naturally to do this, try wearing something subtle on your hands, like nail varnish or cufflinks, which when you notice it will remind you to look up, make eye contact, nod and smile.

- **No rush** Before you answer a question, take a breath, talk more slowly than you think you should and pause every now and again. Nervously gabbling answers in the fashion of someone who has verbal diarrhoea is not going to get you the job.

- **Finish it** It's important to leave the interviewer with a final good impression. If you shuffle off, mumbling and looking awkward, you're doing yourself a disservice. Instead – yet again! – make eye contact, smile, shake hands firmly and tell them you've enjoyed meeting them and that you'd really love the opportunity to work with them.

Public speaking

- **Wear prepared** Plan your outfit ahead of time. Make sure it looks good from different angles, especially from above and below. And it's better to cover up than to inadvertently reveal too much. Go for something that feels appropriate and makes you feel comfortable and like you're being yourself. If you feel confident in black, resist the urge to dress in something flamboyant. Instead, simply perk things up with a couple of colourful accessories. When you've selected something, get a second opinion, just to be sure.

- **No fiddling** Avoid jewellery or accessories that will encourage you to twiddle nervously. Tie your hair back, so you don't play with it. And if you do find yourself fidgeting, try clasping your hands together in the manner of someone who is engaged and concentrating on the matter in hand.

- **Your why** Tap into the reason why you're stepping out onto the stage. Why are you speaking up? Whose life do you want to impact? If you wimp out of giving your talk, what will the consequences be? Who misses out? Knowing that lives will be changed, even if only in a small way, helps us to face down our fears. Giving a talk is not just moving your mouth like a Thunderbirds puppet. There should be emotion and passion in what you're saying. Put your sensitive superpowers to good use and try to connect with the reason behind your words.

- **Look for evidence** Is this the scariest thing you've ever done? Doubtful. What about the time you had a baby? Quit your job? Went bungee jumping? Handled that spider? Moved to a new city? Asked for help? Make a list of the three brave and mighty things you've done before and then tell yourself, I know I can do this because I did that.

- **House of cards** Write your notes on small index-style cards. Aim for just a few key points per card. No long sentences. Your notes are prompts; they're not for reading out verbatim. Long-form notes are very tempting indeed, but you'll get lost and spend the whole time with your head down reading. You need to be able to glance at the cards and know instantly what you want to say. It's also a good idea to link your cards with a string, so that they don't fall all over the floor or get jumbled.

- **Run your lines** Rehearse your talk in front of the mirror . . . lots of times. Go over and over it, so that you know it back to front. Then, when you're ready, do a dry run in front of a friend, too. You're not aiming to recite your talk completely off by heart on the day (unless you want to sound like a robot), but knowing that the words are drummed into your brain will give you an added layer of security – a bit of back-up, should the nerves kick in.

- **Hydration station** Water is your secret speaking weapon, and sipping it will help to calm your nerves and stop your mouth from drying out, so that your words don't get stuck on the sandpaper of your tongue. Plus, taking a sip of water gives you a moment to pause, think and gather your thoughts. Sneaky! Be sure to go easy, though. Use a bottle or a straw, and take little swigs in a delicate fashion to limit the risk of waterboarding yourself mid-talk.

- **Own it** If you're anxious or new to public speaking, it's ok to say so. 'I'm a little nervous, but what I have to say is important. So I'm pushing past my fears!' As well as helping you to feel more comfortable, sharing your feelings with the audience will actually help you to connect with them on a deeper level.

- **People want you to succeed** The audience are your supporters. They want you to do well. You're basically standing up in front of a massive cheerleading squad willing you on. Even if the audience already know the content of what you're saying, you're giving them the chance to reinforce their knowledge.

- **A fresh twist** If you're questioning your level of experience and imposter syndrome has got you by the throat, it's time to get personal: you're the best person – and the only person – who can be you. By sharing your story, experiences and personal perspective, you'll be presenting information in a whole new way.

- **Play the triangle** To avoid getting overwhelmed by a sea of faces in the audience, pick three friendly, smiling ones to speak to. (If you're worried that nobody will be smiling, you could always ask people in advance to smile at you.) Making eye contact will help you to connect with your audience and stop you from being transfixed by the floor or your notes. Choosing one person at the back and one on each side of the audience helps you to shift your gaze and gives the impression that you're commanding the room.

- **Erm . . . No!** If you're not sure how to respond to a question, rather than saying 'Erm . . .' or looking blank, use a phrase like, 'That's a good question', or 'I just need a moment to structure my thoughts', to buy yourself a little more time.

Meetings & Work

- **Encourage online networking** Online platforms that create a social network for organisations with online chat and activity feeds help people stay up to date. Shy people like to communicate in writing, so this kind of thing suits us.

  Alternative feedback methods, like using shared documents and collaboration tools, reduce our reliance on verbal, on-the-spot communication.

- **Manage meetings better** In order to solve the trickiest problems and generate the best ideas, organisations need a mixture of personalities, thinking styles and preferences. And yet, when people get together and start communicating, the quietest voices are often disregarded. And, when it comes to hot air being spouted ad infinitum, by people who like the sound of their own voice rather too much, meetings are notorious. If your meetings are noisy and dysfunctional, it's time to make them more inclusive, and as a result, more productive.

- **Have a word** As a manager, if you know that someone tends to dominate meetings, or talk over others, it's up to you to have a word. Talk to them privately. Mention that in the best interests of the team and your results, you want to make sure everyone is heard.

- **Stick up** If meetings become a bun fight, suggest trying out a new method, like a talking stick or bear or ball or hat: choose one item, preferably not an actual bun or cream cake, this is not a free-for-all, after all. The bear or ball or hat is passed around, and only the person holding the thing can speak. Encouraging this kind of structure benefits everyone, not just shy people.

- **Prioritise preparation** Circulate meeting agendas ahead of time. Give shy people a chance to prepare and think beforehand. I mean, who wouldn't want their people coming to a meeting prepared? It's not meant to be an improvisation exercise. Or a game, where the idea is to spout the most amount of bullshit under pressure. Now there's an image.

- **Break it down** I'm sure we've all been in badly run meetings and brainstorms where the same people shout out their terrible suggestions, while other participants sit in stunned silence. This shouty, stormy method does not generate the best ideas. Fact. Breaking into smaller groups of up to four people, with one scribe per group, is more effective. And you might just uncover some sparks of genius.

- **Think on it** If everyone talks over each other, there's not much thinking going on. After the meeting, or before, let the person in charge know that you'd like to give it some deeper thought, rather than rushing to conclusions, and that you'll come back to them later that day with some ideas or recommendations.

- **Ahead of the game** You could also suggest a team debrief instead of a free for all, where things are submitted ahead of time, perhaps in a shared document that the manager or facilitator goes through during the meeting. Having this ahead of time makes it easier to structure the meeting, anyway. It might even turn out that you don't need to have a meeting, or that it could be limited to just a few minutes.

- **Use silence as a strength** Trial new communication techniques, such as silent meetings, pioneered by the likes of Amazon. At silent meetings, instead of just talking, most of the meeting time is actually spent doing the work. No way! You spend five minutes on the brief, twenty or so minutes thinking and doing and even commenting in writing on a shared document, then regroup for a debrief. People have time to think. And work gets done. Sounds dreamy, doesn't it?

- **Harness anonymity** Crack open the door to innovation and keep it ajar by inviting people to submit ideas and feedback anonymously, via a suggestion box. Bash down bias by allowing anonymity, so all ideas are considered, no matter the status, job title or face fit of the person who suggested them.

- **The power of getting personal** One-to-ones are a marvellous way to encourage people to share their ideas, rather than relying on them to overcome self-consciousness and be able to speak up in front of a group. Give people an option to share, one to one, via email or chat, before or after a meeting. You may find that you uncover previously silent potential.

- **Have a huddle** Discussing or working on a project in a small group is undeniably quieter and more productive than holding large, noisy meetings. If meetings are not your thing, have a quickie huddle with the people who matter most.

- **Shine a light on someone else** Share the success of someone in your team. It can feel awkward talking about your own achievements. But if you talk about the team effort, and mention other people's achievements, while discreetly showing that you were the one steering it all, it's subtle and effective.

- **Buddy up** If you're not a fan of sharing back to the team on your own, team up with someone and share ideas in a pair. Start by just standing with them as they share your combined efforts. Then, over time, build up to saying something, then gradually spending more time talking. Until it's just you.

- **Spotlight talent** Rather than relying on people putting themselves forward for awards, competitions, features in the press or other exposure, encourage a culture of nominations, whereby people celebrate the achievements of others.

- **You're welcome** Help new people to adjust. Shy people need time to get acclimatised to a new situation or team. If things get switched up, or you welcome a new arrival, be mindful that they will need a warming-up period. Once shy people feel comfortable, like they're in a family, they will find speaking up and getting involved easier.

- **Find your niche** Have an idea of what you want to be known for. Don't just let stuff happen to you. Look out for opportunities to shine. If you're not keen on bragging about your own achievements, perhaps you could offer to write an article for the website? Or get involved in a volunteering project? Think about what would work for you, and go after it, rather than feeling frustrated because you don't want to do the stuff everyone else seems to find easy.

- **Goal getter** Be intentional about meetings. Set yourself a mighty mission for every meeting you attend. Perhaps you intend to smile at three people, introduce yourself, say one thing or ask a question. If you hit your goal, don't forget to give yourself a little reward. Boom.

- **Take note** Proper preparation will elevate your meeting game. Don't just rock up and hope for the best. Do your homework and bring any salient points and background information with you. Be a reliable source of knowledge; a fount, if you will.

- **Early bird** Falling through the door, late and frazzled, with all eyes on you, is *so* not a good look. Aim to be a few minutes early. If you're one of the first in the room, people will say hi to you. You can get a sense of who's who and what's what, in a cool, calm, frenzy-free fashion.

- **Be big** It's not just what you say that counts. Body language is important, too. We shy people tend to recoil and hunch, avoid eye contact and bow our heads. It's like we're trying to slide under the table. Instead of shrinking away, make yourself bigger. Spread out, put your papers in front of you, put your hands on the table, sit up straight. Take up space.

- **Precision point** Have an outcome in mind for the meeting. Is there a particular thing you'd like to achieve, an impression you'd like to make, a question you'd like answered or an issue you'd like to draw attention to? Write it down – somewhere you can focus on it throughout the meeting.

- **Lower the bar** Take the pressure off yourself to be perfectly pithy. Shy people may struggle to speak up, whereas others struggle to stop talking. People do talk a load of crap in meetings! So consider the levels of hot air enveloping us all, and know this: you don't need to be an oratory master in order to have a voice.

- **Ask away** If you haven't managed to contribute to the meeting yet, and anxiety is setting in, don't panic. The first step towards getting involved in the conversation is simply to ask a question. Ask for clarification, or an opinion or next steps. Not only is asking a question a pressure-free way to contribute, but a pertinent question has the power to focus a conversation on what's really important.

- **Jump on it** When someone finishes speaking, there will be a lull, even if only for a split second, and that's your chance – your opportunity to speak. If you're waiting for a long, drawn-out silence or a drumroll, you may be disappointed, and if other people have a tendency to interrupt each other, you need to hop in with both feet or you will miss your moment.

- **Get creative** Make meetings more productive by putting all that listening and thinking time to good use. The key is to create something that goes beyond simple notes or minutes – perhaps a mind map, a proforma or set of key questions. Formulate something useful that you can share with the other participants and demonstrate your mighty powers.

- **Careful consideration** Leverage your listening skills. Become known as the person who listens and then, when everyone else has finished waffling on, comes up with a carefully considered point or a fresh perspective. 'Having listened to everyone's opinions, it seems to me . . .' or 'Having weighed up our options, the best course of action appears to be . . .' Be the smart summarising person who separates the meatballs from the spaghetti.

- **Follow up** If you didn't manage to say everything you wanted to say during a meeting, follow up with key people via email. Demonstrate that you've given the matter extra thought – which you certainly will have done!

A FINAL WORD

By now, you are well acquainted with your shyness. Like old friends, you have an understanding. Sure, there are times where you irritate the hell out of each other, but on the whole, you rub along pretty well together.

You've dug into what it's like to be shy, whether you were born shy or it came later, and the things that may trigger your shyness. You've rummaged around in your brain a bit and seen what happens biologically when you feel shy.

You know you are not alone. More than half of us are shy. You are not broken. You don't need fixing. You know that the world needs you to speak up. And that your voice matters.

You are owning your shyness and finally talking about it. Even if it's just a whisper. You don't need to fundamentally change who you are; you know that. And it feels good. Instead, you are embracing your shyness, and working with it.

You feel free! You've disentangled yourself from judgement and kicked comparisonitis to the kerb. And you've started caring a bit more carefully.

Hopefully, too, you're being kinder and more compassionate to yourself; treating yourself like you would treat a best friend. You're taking care of yourself, embracing comfort and finding safety and snuggliness when you need to rest and recover.

You've looked inwards and found that you're stronger than you thought you were.

You've unearthed your shy skills and you're making them work for you.

You've taken control of the situation, shaping the world around you.

You've started to assemble your power team – because you know that with the right kind of people in your corner, you are mighty.

You're ready for action.

From now on you're going to be stepping forward, out of the background, and seizing opportunities. No more being overlooked or underestimated. No more feeling lonely and frustrated. No more missing out.

No more being invisible. From now on, be invincible.

Be shy . . . and mighty!

Nadia x

PS If you'd like to find out more about the Shy and Mighty project, book in some coaching, get the down low about my work in schools and organisations, listen to the Shy and Mighty podcast, or just message me, head over to www.shyandmighty.com – I'd love to hear from you.